Tha Recovering Lesbian

RAINYRAIN MCQUEEN

THA RECOVERING

LESBIAN

BY

RAINYRAIN

MCQUEEN

Cover photo creation by – RainyRain

Photographer – Eric Maxey

Hand Model – Sasha Mone'

Edited by – Self Made Talents

Dedicated to the memory of:

Uncle Nate   Cynadoll

Queen   Billy Maxwell

TyShawn Burkley   RaShaud Biggs

MacAuther Haynes

Geraldine "Pookie" McQueen

WARNING: This book contains Mental Triggers like child abuse, domestic violence, drug usage, sexual violence and Suicide.

PLEASE READ AT YOUR OWN RISK1

The Recovering Lesbian is MY TESTIMONY to all those people who do not understand homosexuality and to those who thought the worst of me and expected me to fail.

Thanks for doing your job.

I would truly like to thank everyone who is everyone important to me in my lifetime through thick and thin. Especially my only wonderful daughter Lil Rain. I prayed to have a girl and God have gave me the best daughter in the world I love you so much. Much love, respect and peace knowing that you cared and believed in me. I pray that no one will ever be offended by my words or thought for they are my own.

A special thanks to Mrs. Roslyn Mahone. A very special dedication and thanks to Latonya Carter thank you for helping me find my way back to Christ and being my study partner, you mean more to me than you know.

A million times THANKS.

To my Baby Momma's Ann, Shela and Tawanna thank you for being my business partner in some shape, form or fashion.

You are my biggest supporters.

Last but not least to all 20 of my children thank you for allowing me to grow as a parent and be a parent with you in some shape, form or fashion.

Love you all equally.

A very extra special dedication to My Future Wife whoever you are

Love you in advance.

CHAPTERS

THE ABUSE

THE FIRST TIME

THE CHILDREN

ADULTHOOD

THUG LIFE

DEATH

SURVIVAL

360 DEGREES

CELL BLOCK

MOVIN FORWARD

L.A

I'M NOT WHO WE THINK I AM

GOING THRU THE MOTIONS

WHERE AM I NOW?

NOW THE JOURNEY REALLY BEGINS

THE ABUSE

Being a lesbian isn't something that happens overnight nor is it something that you just decide to come into. It is a mental process of how you want to receive love. Coming into that notion of how you want to be loved and give love in return starts from your childhood and where you come from. A lot of people like me can honestly say they were born and programmed, that's how I got started. The abuse and programming were set into place when I was in the womb. You see, when my mom was about 7 months pregnant or so, her husband tried to kill her, but my sister stopped him by stepping in the way and talking him out of it. The man was very heartbroken when he found out that I wasn't his baby. It seemed that not only was my mom cheating with my dad, my dad was cheating on his wife with her. It crushed my heart to find out that I was the creep baby

that broke the whole family apart. I am the

seventh baby of my moms' and the baby of my

dads' four and his only daughter. My sperm

donor Lorenzo, never was in my life that I can

remember. I was told that he stopped coming

around when I was four. My mom always told

me who he was and who my half- brothers were,

I even had pictures of them all, his address and

phone number. I guess she always made sure

that I was able to reach out to him if I wanted to.

   With my mom being divorced and my dad

running back and forth from Canton, OH to

Youngstown, OH, I guess it was too much for

him to have two women, so he paid child

support and split. Now it's true when they say

hurt people, hurts people and I was the one who

got hurt. My dad leaving gave the same hurt to

my mom that she gave to her husband and she couldn't handle it. I look just like my dad and his side of the family. So raising and looking at someone who is a constant reminder of the person who hurt you, can become too much for a person. As I was growing up I got yelled at or hit for every little thing I did wrong. By the time I reached five I knew how to organize my toys, clean, peel potatoes and make my bed military style and she really bounced the quarter on the bed.   The first day of my life that I can really recall was in 1980.

It was the first day of kindergarten and all my clothes were laid out on my bed. I was so excited to go specially to get away from a brother who tends to annoy me all my life. I remember it like it was yesterday, my mom and I headed off to Hillman Elementary. I had on a pink blouse with the tie up string, a silky black skirt with white

ruffle socks and black patented leather shoes with

the strap across the top of the shoe. I got to class a

little nervous but happy. I kissed my mother

good-bye and went to sit down next to a boy I

thought was cute. The bell rang, and class was

ready to begin. Everything was fine beside the

cold I only felt throughout my legs. I paid the cold

no mind and continued to listen to what Mrs. Ross

was saying. I'd say about an hour had went by

when suddenly there was a knock at the

classroom door, it was my mother, I felt so

embarrassed because I thought she missed me and

wanted me to come home even though I wanted

to stay. My teacher stepped out into the hallway

with my mother and was gone no less then fifteen

seconds. Mrs. Ross came back in and told me to go

talk to my mother and I can come straight back

when I am done. When I got outside my mom grabbed my arm and headed straight to the bathroom. Now I admit by this time I just knew I was getting a whooping for something my brother did. She pulled my skirt up, I closed my eyes and tried to prepare myself for this pain that I was about to experience and then she spoke "Lorraine, you forgot to put your panties on, here". I opened my eyes with a sigh of relief; I threw my panties on and jetted to class.

My mother was the perfect house mom. She always made sure all seven of us were well dressed, respectable and stayed in school. Hell, bringing home a diploma or getting married was the only way to get out of the house. She always made sure I never saw her drink, smoke, or have a boyfriend around me, wish I could say that for my siblings. They called me my mom's shadow. All the kids were grown and had their own family and kids. The baby boy was eight years older, so it was just me and him growing up half of my life. Our bills were always paid by the fifth of the month and she loved going to flea markets, garage sales and digging in the rich folk's trash. Martha Stewart didn't have anything on my mom when she hooked all that second-hand stuff up. I really loved my mom and would do anything to make her proud, but sometimes my anything would mean trouble for me.   The street we stayed on was full of boys and maybe about ten girls. Now the majority of the girls in the neighborhood were teenagers. I was the middle child of my neighborhood and my cousins. Therefore, I was too young to play with some and too old to play with others. I loved to ride my bike and play football; in fact, I liked it so much that when it got hot I would take my shirt off like the boys did.

What did I do that for? My mother saw me and beat my tail like there was no tomorrow, I was only seven years old. After a few beatings I stopped taking off my shirt and just sweated terribly.

We finally got cable and for the first time ever I saw a man and a woman in the bed naked, kissing, rubbing and laying all over each other. I didn't understand it, but I knew I shouldn't be watching it so I changed the channel. A few days later the boy across the street named Henry and I was in my back yard playing because it was raining in the front yard, it used to do that from time to time, I guess u can say that God was our sprinkler system in the summer.

We were tired of running around the house and were still wet from playing up front, so

Henry decided to make up a new game called T.V. I didn't know how to play so I asked what I had to do. He pulled me into a corner in the back of the house and told me to pull my pants down. I didn't ask I just did it. Then he said he was about to pee on me. I panic "No you're not this is not a game Henry". "Sike!" said Henry. "It was something I saw on TV. So, he pulled me closer and when I realized this is what I saw on T.V I opened my legs wider, so he can put his little peter where I saw them on TV put it.

Someone yelled very loud and angrily, "Lorraine!" I jumped and peeked around the corner and saw my mother. Now Henry ran home and left me for dead. I was trying to run to but before I could bust a move my mom busted my ass. Now here's the thing about my mom when you're in trouble, you're in trouble. That day when my mom finally got tired of whooping me with the belt she went to her hand then back to the belt, all this lasted for an hour or so. Not to mention she was carrying my little nephew in her arms the whole time. When the beating was done my mom took me across the street to Henry's house and told his mother. Then came another whooping because they switched and beat the skin off both of us. I wasn't allowed outside for a month.   I noticed that I wasn't done being curious about stuff because I began to wonder how boys used the bathroom in a different way than girls. So, me being the experimental one used the bathroom backwards. It never seemed to fail, I guess moms are built with radar because here comes mine in the bathroom; "Lorraine!" What the hell are you doing?

You're not a boy; I'm tired of this shit." So, as you

can imagine there goes another beating this one

lasted longer, and I couldn't do anything but sleep

when she was done.   When I woke up for dinner

I guess she was so disgusted in me for what I had

done and for looking like my father, mom looked

at me, rolled her eyes and said "Lorraine" do u

know what a dyke is?

"No Ma'am,"

"Well it's you! You aren't going to be shit but a

dyke." From then on you can say I was

programmed.   Every weekend my mom

and her sisters would go to the clubs and meet

up with some of their friends. I always had to

stay home with my brother who was eight

years older than me. Since he was my brother I

thought it was cool at the time that he would let

me stay up late and watch my three favorite

shows Benny Hill, Solid Gold, and Soul Train.

My brother Ralph hated watching me on the weekend because he wanted to go fishing with his dad, but mommy said: "No you must stay here and watch your little sister!"   I myself began to dislike my brother because if I wanted to stay up late and watch my shows I would have to lay in front of the television, while he grinded on me until I felt something warm on my back. By that time Soul Train was about to come on, I'd then go to the bathroom to clean up and make it back down stairs to watch it. He'll send me to my room when the show was over.   One day my brother was in the restroom and I was in my room playing when he called for me to come here. I got up and went into the hallway, to my surprise he had his penis sticking out the door. He told me to suck it or he'll beat me up, I did it for about two seconds then bit

the fuck out of him. He never touched me again.

Well my mom caught me again, grinding the

couch this time. When she asked me where I got

the idea from, being scared to tell it was my

brother and the fact that she believed I was such

this big liar, I lied and said the teenage boy across

the street. I got a beating and he went to J.J.C. Like

I said before pleasing my mom always meant

trouble for me.

Ever since I can remember I have been called

an asshole, bitch, dyke, hoe, slut, dumb, stupid and

tramp.

You name it I was called it. I still love my mom to
death,

I'm supposed to. It wasn't until I got older that I

realized I had been verbally abused. With my

mom who always managed to hurt my feelings

one way or another, my brother molesting me and my sister treating me like crap because she had to watch me a lot. My mom would leave me with my sister Punkin and her husband Norman sometimes for months at a time. I guess you can say I was abused in every direction and it was the start of something that I surely was not ready for in my future.

Lord please help me to be as strong as David, as wise as Solomon, and as precious as Jesus in everything

I do.

~UNKNOWN~

THE FIRST TIME

By the time I was thirteen my brother Ralph went off to college thank God! I was the only child left in the house. When I turned thirteen I thought that it meant I could make my own decisions on what I could eat and wear. I found out that I had another thing coming.

The day after my thirteenth birthday, my friends Loretta and Blossom decided to get this boy Skeet I liked a lot to strip for me as a birthday present. When he was done, I lost my virginity and began to really get into boys. I was a "C" average student who was quiet, yet a class clown and had a knack for poetry. Between the time I first got into Junior High and High School, I have won ten after school fights, two hallway fights and lost only once. I never was an instigator nor liked to get into trouble. I was cool until someone pushed my buttons.

Once that happened I blacked out and I had one hitter quitters, they used to call me Mrs. Tyson.

By the ninth grade everyone knew I wasn't the one to mess with unless you had a good reason and ready to give it your all. I remember the main reason everyone thought I was crazy in junior high. We were in music class and this girl Stacy tore up a sheet of paper into small pieces and started sprinkling them in my hair. I told her to stop and when she didn't. I jumped up and punched her. The teacher came, and we were escorted to the office. Now on the way out the class I pushed on the swinging doors a little too hard because my hand went through the glass doors. I didn't mean to do that, but it happened. I did not realize I was hurt until the

Principal was running water over my hand and it started burning.

I got six stitches that day and a three-day suspension.

The most difficult time I had in junior high was dealing with the peer pressure, criticisms and my tomboyish ways. Even then people thought I was a lesbian. I engaged in track and basketball. Every day after practicing me, Loretta and Blossom would go over one of our boyfriends' house get drunk and had sex. When I went home I made like I was so exhausted from practice that I would eat, wash up and go straight to sleep. My mom never had a clue of my after-school activities.

It was not until that next spring and six sex partners later, that my sexual emotions were far out of control and unexplainable.

I remember walking down the hall on my way to third period, when I saw this girl who was so pretty to me. I found myself staring at her. I played it off and kept heading to class. On my way I was wondering to myself why was I staring and felt so weird inside about this girl. By the time sixth period came I was stunned to see the same girl in class with me. I sat in the back of the class, so no one would see me staring at her and smiling. I could not understand why I was so interested in this girl so much. When school was over I saw one of my older cousins waiting for her god daughter. I stopped to talk to her and before I could finish my conversation. The same girl who I liked was the god daughter she was waiting on. From then on, we all walked home together after school, go to her house watch Duck Tales and took a nap before her mom came home from work. Since I was cool with all the boys who wanted her, they always wanted me to hook them up with her. I admit that if I didn't like the guy I would mess it up so she wouldn't give them a chance. One day Jason who sat next to me passed a note asking me to help him write a poem for her because he's not that good at it and he loved the one I wrote for class. I told him yes all because I wanted to use him to say what I wanted to say to her in the first place. I thought it was a clever idea and we would get a poem to her once a week. Little did I knew then, that those poems would be the beginning of a beautiful relationship because on those walks home I would get the chance to hear how she really felt about my words and feelings. I want to tell her so bad that I was in love with her but at that time it wasn't acceptable to date the same sex.

As the years past we became very close. We hung out, fought and got suspended together. We lived together, raised our kids together, everything. Whenever you saw her you saw me.

It wasn't until my twenty-first birthday that I told her all these years in my mind she was my girlfriend and how I had always wanted to be with her. Even though we both had boyfriends she was my first true love for a person. So, when she agreed to sleep with me, I felt like I was on top of the world.

Even though we maintain a wonderful friendship until this day. For seventeen years of my life in my mind no matter who I was with or what I was doing. She was my girlfriend and my first love. I had expectations I shouldn't have. Now I have no choice but to face these emotions that I myself cannot explain, but in the meantime here goes nothing.

The experience that helped me to become comfortable with the feelings I had inside about the same sex and me, was with an older woman a week before my 21st. She was a sister of a classmate and I gave her a ride to the grocery store and on the way back she came on to me with her foot up on my dash board and we went to my place and I lost my virginity to my first woman

Expectations is like a drug. The first time you do what everyone expects you to do. They're hooked.

~unknown~

THE CHILDREN

After getting my mom approval of having a boyfriend, only because she knew his family. My mom never knew I was having sex until she notices that I hadn't had my period in two months. My mom took me to the doctor and when he told her that I was pregnant. My mom flipped out on me. On the walk home from the doctor. My mom curses me out and told me I was going to have to eat my baby. I cried the whole way home and beg my mom not to make me eat my baby. The closer I got to home, the more I became frightened. We walked in the house and mama grabbed up a fork and knife and told me to sit at the kitchen table and to start cutting and eat my baby. I cried and begged her to let me go and that I will take care of my baby on my own. Just please don't make me eat it. That's when I got up and tried to run out the house, but she grabbed me by the arm and started slapping on me.   She told me to shut up and that I will finish school, even if I have to take my baby to school with me. Trust I did just that. I went to school every day until it was time for me to deliver. Now, by this time when I had my first child I was 16 and in 10th grade. Now the father was older than me. He had a car, was a senior, had bracelets' and was a total asshole. When I told him, I got pregnant that night when the hole in his car got us soaked from the rain and I dried my cloths at his house (we had sex and he claim he had a rubber on and even though it lasted for 90 seconds), He denied it.

My mom knew his parents and tried to talk to him about how he needed to step up and take responsibility for his child. Till this day no love or contact with my son. I gave Mom an A for effort but, fuck him.

I was two weeks late and had to have my labor induced. While I was in labor my baby daddy had the nerve to bring his girlfriend to the hospital. I was so angry I started pulling my IV out of my arm and jumped out the bed but my mom stopped me before I could punch him in the face. My mom asked him to leave and come back with his mom and aunt.

I was in labor for eighteen hours. He was 8 pounds and 9 ounces. I had Dominique Tarell two weeks after my sixteenth birthday with sixteen stitches. He was the biggest, head full of hair and beautiful baby in the whole hospital. The

nurses had my baby all the time. I used to have to

ask for my baby back. It did not help that one of

my aunts worked at the hospital on my

floor.

When I brought my baby home. I had so

much stuff it lasted me two months. By the time

he was two months, my sister gave me a baby

shower.   The funniest time I had with my

son was when he learned how to climb out of

the walker. He used to mess with my mom nick

knacks on her shelf. I used to get yelled at and

in so much trouble for those things being out of

place. One day Dominique was a little too quiet

so when I went to check on him. I found him in

his walker upside down. His head was too

heavy. It seemed that he was climbing out to

bother things and then climb back in when he hears someone coming.

He was so smart sometimes he was too smart for his own good.

When I did my homework, I would do my homework with my son I would read my books to him.   He was a good kid. He was potted trained at eight months and never peed in the bed. He was just sneaky as hell. I struggled with him because my mom was upset of how good I was handling school and a child. So, she told me that she was not going to watch him anymore while I go to school.

So being a good teenage mom I took him to school with me. Three days later my principal Mr. Bentley called me into his office and told me I had to find a babysitter. School policy will not allow me to bring him anymore. So once the school called; my mom started watching him again but at a cost. I had to pay rent and a bill to continue staying with her or she was going to put me and my child out on the streets. She also made it clear that I could not stay with any family members or she was going to beat me up. Things finally calmed down between us until my mom found out she was a diabetic. So, every morning before school I got my baby dress, bottles made and gave her insulin shot and breakfast. When I came home from school I repeated the same thing and did my homework.

Now by eleventh grade I was pregnant again. This time I covered my tracks, so I tried to cover it. I found out I was pregnant when his father called me from jail and said he has been vomiting to bad and I should check and find out.

When I took that test my poor heart stopped.

How my mom was going to kill me was all I can think about. I have been selling weed since eighth grade so now, I knew I had to double up. I do not believe in abortions, but I was willing to take the risk than go up against my mom. I tried to be civil about it and with the help of a teacher I went to court and had a judge grant me permission to have an abortion without my mom consents and to emancipate myself from her.

A day before my appointment my mom was snooping in my room and found the money I had saved. I was so scared, and I was far pass trying to lie. I knew my mom was going to take my money regardless. So, when I told her what it was for and I showed her the court papers.

I got my face slapped and a few blows to the stomach. She told me since I want to be grown and do shit without her I was going to have this baby and that she was not helping me with it and when I graduate pack my stuff and get out.

Now it's 1993 my senior year and so much has happened. South High School was closing, and our senior class would be the last graduating class since 1912. Even though I was pregnant I still tried to have as much fun as a senior I could have. I was on the yearbook and newspaper staff. I participate in our Gong

Show which is like the Apollo. I did Bobby Brown song

Get

Away and I was on the South High variety show staff. The variety show was something we have every year that shows our town school kids talents and imagination and it was ran and hosted by the seniors of that year. The day of the variety show I just knew I was going to see all our hard work pay off. As I was getting dress

for the last special event in my senior life before,

my water broke.

I was so upset because I wanted to go to the

show and I was two weeks early. My mom drove

me to the hospital and at the same time the show

started I had Eric Alonzo 7pounds, 15 ounces and

22 ½ inches long. His dad didn't make it because

my mom did not like him and didn't call him until

afterwards. After I had Eric and seen he was ok I

tried to sneak out to go to the show, but my mom

caught me. I had Eric in April, graduated 56th in my

class with two children and moved out with his

dad three days after graduation.

My mom kept her promise and she never

helped me with Eric she wouldn't even hold him.

The one time she did hold Eric I took a picture of it

and she covered her face in that. I guess not

holding him was her way of not getting close and

helping me with him.

 Three years have passed and by this time I found

out I was pregnant again and only my best friend

knew

about it.

My mom had just passed and it brought out

a lot of bad words and feelings between my older

sister Gerl and me and us fist fighting didn't help

our sorrow. That fight, mom passing, along with

being five months pregnant in my tubes and a

cheating ass boyfriend cause me to have a

miscarriage. The doctor told my best friend Ann

that I was hemorrhaging so bad another thirty

minutes and I would have died. I named him

Dexter Scott. Losing him gave me a nervous

breakdown and several suicide attempts. None the

less with all that was going on around me, my most

inner battle that I was having with myself was my lust for women as it grew even more each day that pass. After all the counseling I and the kids went thru. It took us six years to completely feel like a normal family again.

After all that and the grief and relief at the same time. I felt like I didn't have to beg for my mom or anyone's approval about nothing. So not only did I get wild I also decided that I was bi-sexual and there's nothing anyone can say about it. I partied and sold weed all night and slept all day. I was so unstable in the mind and heart.

When me and my boyfriend Tim finally broke up after five years of cheating and 2 STD's I ran into this guy named Lenny at the drive thru who flashed his money and played like this sweet guy. I fell for it and before I knew it I was pregnant again. This time I had spent so much time with my best friend daughter that I prayed to have a daughter of my own, so I knew the moment I got pregnant it was a girl. I even bet some of my friends and family it was a girl that's how I bought all her baby stuff.

 While I was pregnant I had the worse evening sickness ever. I used to smoke a joint just to make myself fall asleep. During the eighth month of my pregnancy. My grandma called Mother's Day morning and asked me to take her to the grocery store around noon. I told her I'll be there with bells on. Noon rolled around, and I called the house. My brother answered the phone. I said, "Tell grandma I'll be there when I get the kids dress and on their school bus." He said "Ok". I hang up the phone.

About an hour later and when I was on my way out the door the phone rang. I started not to answer the phone, but something told me to go and answer it. It was my Niece Marlena. Grandma was dead. Again, more family drama between my aunts and my older sister over money.

The kicker of it all was by us cleaning the house getting ready for the funeral. All I was doing was inhaling a lot of lead dust straight to my baby. My grandma has been in that house I believe since the 60's. So, when 7 pounds 8 ounces Tim-Echa Bo'Zett was born six weeks later, she had so much lead poisoning in her system that the hospital kept her for a week and shaved the sides of her head to put an I.V in it. The lead poison had us at the doctors every week for blood test. My baby was only one and got stuck so much she use to just roll up her own sleeve and put her arm out for the nurse. We used to try every trick in the book to get her to take her medicine which had such a horrible smell. I used to cry because I had to force her to take it. If you never knew how serious lead poison can be. Let me tell you that if she caught the slightest cold, her fever will go up to 102 and then here come the seizures. She has been hospitalized for a week about four times. She even once was in a coma for a month and again for a week. She was about three when she was finally lead free and the seizures stopped.   Now I have 17 other children that I claim. I got three with Ann, Three with Shela, Three with Shun, Five with L.A, two of my birth kid's best friends who been around forever Bee Bee and Diego, and a very special daughter I calls Mudders.

Now why is Mudders so special? Let me tell you. Mudders was my cousin god daughter and for whatever reason Mudders was about two to three months old and was staying with my

cousin and her kids. I always stopped by after

work to wind down before I went home because

of the problems me and my wife was having. The

moment I laid my eyes on her, I picked her up,

smiled gave her a kiss and said, "Look at the little

Mudders, Cuddy who baby you stole? She is so
cute and adorable."

From that point on my mission was to not wind

down but spend time with Mudders, we had an

instant connection. She knew it too because after

that once I came over she would cry if anyone else

held her. They used to have to call me over to put

her to sleep. Now mind you I never meet the

mother of this child, we both used to just hear

about each other. When me and Tawana did meet

Mudders was about six months old.

Tawana and my cousin fell out and Mudders was gone. That broke my heart. I had no one to put a little sunshine in my life before I deal with my problems of marriage. I did everything I could to track her down and when I did. It took eight phone calls six messages and finally Tawana comes to my house to see me and we sat and talked and got to know each other. I had to ensure her that I am nothing like my cousin and that her baby will be safe in my care. She started bringing Mudders around and when she got comfortable enough Mudders was with me all the time everyone in my family and at my job knew who Mudders was. Tawana would work the grave yard shift and I worked in the morning so she did not have to worry about a sitter because I had her.

Mudders even had her own Christmas at my house. Lil

Rain enjoyed having a little sister around and she loved Lil Rain. Tish enjoyed her too, but I think she was a little jealous because Mudders had a big amount of my attention. I went to meet my grandson Cameron for the first time because I left Texas a few months before he was born, and he was turning two years old. So, I took Mudders and her mom to Texas with me to meet the rest of my family. So even my Texas family know about my Mudders and we all love her so much. She has a smile and spirit that is so contagious, you can't help but to fall in love with her. Till this day I still talks and send my child support when I can for her. Anything Mudders need I am just a phone call away. Me and Tawana grew a wonderful friendship and she accepts me as her baby daddy of Mudders. As time went we grew so much that if a man she is dating piss her off I get the man bashing cussing out for what he did. I always ask her if she wants me to beat them up and that always makes her feel better that someone wants to help heal her pain and listens to her problems. Tawana even invested in A.W.R.P financially. I will always love here through thick and thin.

Out of all my kids Mudders and L.A kids have always accepted me like a Dad in their life and I love them for accepting me as I am and who I was. I hope they all know that I will always care, love and support them whether they see it or not.

A parent's love is like Jesus love. It never fails.

~unknown~

ADULTHOOD

When you become a so-called adult. The

first thing you think is how fun, fulfilling and

rewarding being on your own can be. I believe my

mom hated that the most about me because I wouldn't call or depend on her for nothing and all I was really trying to do was not burden her knowing she was sick.

Around mid-January in 1995, my mom diabetes got worse and she needed to be in a nursing home. She really did not like that idea very much. Once that happened she made me promise that when things get more complex to let her die no life support and to make sure she doesn't suffer like her father did with the disease and to put gloves on her hand. She did not like the way her hands looked. Take care of her house and tell my oldest child she loves him.

That March the doctor called for a meeting about my mom. It turned out to be a big blow out with me, my mom and older sister Gerl. The doctor told us straight out that if she goes home she will be dead in a month. I hated

the fact of my mom in a nursing home, but what

can I do. They can give her the care that I can't

any more.

My mom was slick one day and she called

my sister-in-law Linda and told her she was

released from the home and to come pick her up. I

get off work and arrived home to my mom sitting

in the wheel chair in the living room.

 After a small argument I did what I had to do and

took care of my mom. I went and got her a walker,

hospital bed, food and briefs. Me and a few of my

friends Ann and Mike helped me lift my mom and

clean her. Who knows where all the rest of my

sisters and brothers were at? Every day that she

was there all my mom fussed about was her house

and accusing me of sleeping with girls. Yes, I may

have had the thoughts but never went any further

with it at that time. She died three weeks later.

Before I left the hospital, I was so hurt. I kissed my

mom on her head, cheeks and feet, then speed off

home. On the way home all I can think about is that

she died with a bad thought of me in her head.

When I finally got home and lay down I just prayed

that this nightmare would end but then things just

seemed to fall downhill from there.

My roommate's ex-boyfriend showed up

unannounced and he saw her with another guy. He

flipped and started jumping on her. I was already

upset about my mom passing so, I took my

frustration out on him and beat him up.

The next morning, I realized it was not a

dream and I am motherless. That's when my

older sister Gerl comes over and started talking

about how she promised mommy she was going

to kick my ass. I couldn't figure out why. I was

the one who changed her diaper, medicated and prepare the proper food for her and she came to kick my ass. That's my older sister and I love her I didn't want to fight. I tried walking away, but she followed me to my sister Punkin house. Gerl came with her husband, step son and his nephew and they came with guns. So, my friend made a call and we were all at my sister house packing our guns and ready to fight. Thank God no one got seriously hurt and all that became of it was a fist fight between me and my sister.

If this is the beginning of adulthood I don't want to grow up. I rather stay a teenager. When things settled down I began to really say fuck everything and my thoughts of women grew stronger. I even tried church, but the flesh beat me up bad. Let's not forget that my twenty-first birthday I slept with my first girl and after that an older woman approached me and I slept with her.

Now I know for a fact that I like sleeping with

women. My mom was gone; I lost a baby and just

went insane with all my feelings and anger. How

do I tell my family and friends that I'm gay?

If this is adulthood I don't want to grow up. Lord

help me through this before I kill someone or

myself.

Faith chooses our relatives. We choose our friends.

-Jacques Delille-

THUG LIFE

What is thug life? I never understood the concept of it. Yet I had my share of the life style. It all began when my nephew who said he was becoming a Crip. I tried to talk him out of it, but I couldn't, so I joined myself. Just so I could keep an eye on my nephew.   When you love your family, you feel that no one can take care of, nor look out for your love ones like you can. The lifestyle I was living was far from a thug I was just emotionally scared and had no clue of how to handle my situations or get help for my pains. So, I threw myself into the Insane Gangsters Crips.

Being a gang member took its toll. My house was decked out in all blue. I had most of our parties. I had responsibility over twelve girls and all I ever did was to party and stay close to my family.

After a while gang banging soon took over and became the theme of the seasons. I watched kids I was two to five years older than, being killed over a colored scarf. I went to two funerals in 1994, seven in 1995 and twenty-two in 1996. That year funeral cloths became your everyday attire. Each month there was something to learn and cry about. It was like all the younger generation just went plum mad. Killing was an everyday thing like using the bathroom. The death that just caught everybody by surprise was a former gang member Ritchie who was 18 and decided to change his ways. He was a basketball star, honor student, got baptized and enrolled into the Army.

He was shot seventeen times over a girl he turned down.

Ritchie was my nephew best friend and my best friend

Ann was engaged to him. His funeral was the first time I ever saw white people at a black person funeral and it were a lot of them. From teachers to students. He had full military honor. At the funeral my best friend gripped the casket so hard and started shaking. I just knew she was about to knock it over. I managed to get her loose and escorted her outside to get some air. It used to be fifteen of us who all hung out together and with Ritchie gone were down to ten and still counting.

All the deaths made me stay closer to my nephew to ensure he won't be the next funeral. As a teenager and young adult growing up in Youngstown, Ohio being killed was normal. Everyone just prayed that they made it through to see another day. At one point we were the

murder capital of the year we even beat

California homicide rate in 1996. The most

horrific death was my cousin friend who was at

the wrong place at the wrong time because they

were shooting at someone else and it caused for

her to get her face blown off with a 12 gauge.

They had to remake a new

face for the funeral.

I even went to jail for assault because my

friend got into an altercation with this girl and I

was high and didn't care, so I jumped in and I

broke the girl nose. Now when the girl tried to

press charges before the arrest. Me and my

friend skipped town and moved to Virginia. I

only returned to sell all my belongings and get

my boys, but it caught up with me and I got

pregnant with the daughter I prayed for, so I

ended up staying in Youngstown and going to jail.   It wasn't until 1998 that all the gang killings began to slow down finally. The thing that slowed me down the most and gave me a moment of clarity was visiting my moms' gravesite and noticing two graves.

On the left was a former Crip member and right next to him was a former blood member. Seeing these two graves made me realize how stupid it was to fight about a color that neither of us own. Killing each other over things in which we completely lost sight of what its true intentions of the gangs starting up in the first place. All while lying next to your so-called enemy for eternity.

Stupid isn't it?   With all that was going on. I was still scared to tell my family I was gay. I was also dealing with the uncontrollable urges to look at women in a sexual manner. So, I covered it by sleeping with all these different guys, dressing like a female and wearing makeup.

That was my thug life. Don't get me wrong I was not innocence. All I was trying to do was learn how to survive in a world that you simply can't survive in, by hiding behind a mask, selling whatever, parting and attending funerals.

Do not go where the path may lead. Go instead where there is no path and leave a trail.

-Ralph Waldo Emerson-

DEATH

When you hear the word death. What does

it mean to you? I remember Jessie Jackson Jr. came

to Youngstown State University to speak to us

high school kids about choices in our life. There was one thing that he said to us that stick with me still to this day.

"When you die your headstone has your name, the date of birth and the date of death. Everything else you have done in your life is represented by that dash in the middle. What do that dash means to you?" His words made me think of life in a whole new way. I truly understand now.

Thank You Mr. Jackson.

Seeing death right before your eyes on a regular basis is not human. We were made to love not make war. The first time I saw death come right before my eyes was when me and my brother Lonnie who every day in the mid-morning would watch M.A.S.H, smoke a joint and talk about life. It was April 1st and he told me out the blue that he was going to die before his birthday and that I was going to be there. I laughed thinking it was an April fool's joke. Every day after that he told me the same thing. When I finally asked him why I got to be there. He said "I need to grow up and take more responsibility for myself. When April 26th came around I went to visit my brother as usual. And as I was walking up the drive way I could hear my brother breathing heavy from the front room. When I got in the house I asked him was he alright. He shook his head no. I asked him if he wanted to go to the hospital. When he said yeah. I knew something was wrong. Lonnie did not like hospitals. He was an alcoholic and had alcoholic seizures. He messed up his leg and had to get surgery and pins in his leg because of a seizure. He left the hospital the moment he

could move. He had been on a walker since.

He asked me to get him some fresh cloths

and under wear from his room. He washed

himself up and got dress. He grabbed his wallet

and I helped him up to get him to my car. I had

the car door open and before I could get half way

there. My daughter, then three and a half, was

on the side of me. I looked down to see where

she was at, so we wouldn't trip over her and I

saw my baby eyes get real wide. My brother

collapsed in my arm. I laid him down and told

my son to call 911. I didn't know C.P.R then. I

was crying and begging him not to die on me.

His eyes were rolling in his head and the sun

was beaming in his face. I took his hat and use it

as shade for his face. By the time the ambulance

got there he was dead. His birthday was April 28th. He was 44 years old.

I had a sign that death was going to be around me a lot more when three of my mother in law five kids passed. I read all their obituary and wrote a poem for their funerals.

The death that got to me the most was when I was working in a nursing home and one of my residents hit his call light. I go to the room and the man looked up at me with a trash can in his hand. He began throwing up chunks of blood everywhere. I yelled for my nurse and I tried to get his head up in fear that he would fall out the bed or choke. The nurse dialed 911 and assisted me in lifting him up on the bed. All the while blood was gushing out his mouth and nose in huge chunks. He died with my hand holding up his head. Now he had a pace maker and it cause his body to jerk even after he was dead. We screamed when it first happened as me and another nurse aide was cleaning him up for the coroner. I since then watched several patients die in my arms or right before my eyes.   The closest I came to death myself besides in the womb was twice. The first time I was hanging out with my cousin Rodell and some more people. Rodell began playing with a sawed-off shotgun and pointing it at us sitting on the couch. I felt very uncomfortable and told him to stop, he said the safety was on and to chill out. Just as I decided to move off the couch, the gun went off and left a hole in the couch right where I was sitting. I peed my pants and went home, I was only 14.

The second time was when I finally got the nerve to confront the woman that I was sharing my man with.

My boyfriend was not too happy with that, he left me threatening notes in my house for two days. I knew by the words on the note that I was in for a ride with him. All I wanted was for him to go his own way and leave me alone. I guess he thought that because I was younger that I was easily fooled, well I was his fool off and on for four years. I didn't know what to do so I went to my Uncle Nate and he had me call the police and report the threats. Now Uncle Nate had me do this both times that he left the notes. Then my Uncle gave me a gun and said, "If that mother fucker hit you, shoot his ass and don't let him take it away from you."   Its Halloween night and I place a stick behind my door so he couldn't get in, since he refused to give me my key back.

Now being the man that he was, he kicked in my

door and started arguing with me while I was

lying on my couch in the basement. The whole

time he was talking I had my gun cocked and

was praying that I didn't have to hurt him. I still

loved him, I was just hurt.   I am the type of

person that talks with my hands, so when he

noticed that I didn't move from my spot under

the cover, he removed the cover and when he

saw the gun. He asked me was I going to shoot

him. I said to him, "If I have to, I just want you

to leave me alone." He looked at me and said,

"Bitch you're not going anywhere".

I felt a cold chill go through me as if he just

slapped the taste out my mouth. I looked up at

him and then my finger had a mind of its own and

that's when I pulled the trigger. I was frozen stiff

with fear for a second and was awakened by his voice yelling, "Bitch you shot me!"

I just knew he was about to kill me in front of my kids because they were in the same room asleep on the couch. I knew it was either him or me and I remember what my momma used to say how the other person look better dead than you do.

I went to pull the trigger again, but we began to tussle over the gun. I pulled the pin out of the 22 Dillinger and let go of it. He took the gun and began to hit me all in my head with it and kicked me quite a few times. When he stopped hitting me he grabbed my little black and white 13-inch television and threw it at me. I thought it was strange that I caught it in my hands with no problem. He left the house but not before he smashed out my driver side back window.

It wasn't until the police came that I found out I shot him, when the officers showed me the trail of blood going down my steps. I grazed him in the head. I guess my prayers for him saved him. Lord knows I never had and never wanted to kill anyone. That incident alone made me fear guns. The main thing that made me really dislikes guns and Halloween. I thank God for protecting my children that day, I could have gotten us all killed. When I showed up to court, I found out that he went to his baby momma for help that night and when she talked mess to him, he beat her up too, so we both ended up in court getting our restraining orders against him. I came to find out that not only was he messing with me, he was still seeing his baby momma and the woman I caught him with and he use to jump on them regularly. I never saw that side of him other than that night.

He was sentenced to one year of probation and

Six months of anger management classes. My

speech hasn't been the same since. Now I

combine my sentences sometimes when I talk to

people.   I saw him two years later because

I happened to move three doors down from his

baby momma. He came to my door and asked

to speak to me and that he doesn't want to hurt

me. I stepped outside to hear what he had to

say. He began by telling me how sorry he was

for what happened and that he hope I could

forgive him. I was good to him and he messed

up. He then asked me to talk to my son Eric

because he is not going to know what he looks

like in ten years and he don't want any trouble.

I was puzzled until he told me that my son

continued to tell him that he remembers what

he did to me and that he was going to get him

when he gets older. You see during our confrontation Eric was holding his four-month old sister on the couch and witness the whole thing. The biggest part was when I moved from that house I found the bullet under the couch they were sitting on from where it had ricochet from a pipe in the basement. I told him I would talk to him and he would not have to worry about him saying anything to him ever again. I saw that man maybe once after that.

I am one of those people who have vivid dreams and talks to the dead sometimes. They were never scary or asks me to do anything wrong or stupid. It would be people I actually knew, and they would come to get a message delivered or to warn me about something that is about to happen to me.

Over the years I have also learned another side of death and that's suicide and spiritual messages. Suicide has also become an epidemic, people of all ages are killing themselves left and right. I do not understand it even though I had several attempts myself, I still can't understand why we think like this.

After me and my son Eric dad broke up. He moved with his mom and I stayed in the apartment we were in. I have never stayed on my own before, so I got a little scared there by myself with the boys, so I decided to get a gun. My nephew friend came by with a thirty-eight special chrome handle. I told him to come back in two days and I will have the money for it. The next day he played Russian roulette with the gun and died. I wish I had the money that day maybe he still would have been here. It seems liked it was the season for dying because around that time people was dying left and right playing that dumb ass game.

I was even awakened by the touch of someone's' hand over mines a long time ago when Dominique was little. I sat up and watched my hand lift and began to wave over my son while he is asleep. When I realize I was not doing it on my own my hand dropped. That morning family called and said my cousin Jeanine killed herself playing the same game. It was during Christmas season and all I could ask myself is why? As you can see I lost a few people to suicide but the one that hits my soul was my friend Chynadoll. She was beautiful had so much talent with dancing and can sing her behind off. Why she killed herself, exactly a year and some change after her best friend Queen was beaten to

death and thrown into some abandoned

road. Do not know. She left us all clueless. I can

say that God showed her it wasn't her time

because the first shot went through her jaw.

Why she pulled the trigger again? When you get

that answer please let me know.

I even remember when a friend of the

family killed himself. It was the night before his

funeral and I had this dream:

I was standing outside the church with

my niece and two nephews, when he comes

outside to join us. I look at him and said," Dude

ain't you supposed to be laying down in that

casket what are you doing out here?" As I was

talking to him the make up over the hole in his

head was melting. He says," Shit it's hot in there,

fuck that, no one really here yet anyways." We

all laugh and then I asked him why he kill

himself. He looked me dead in the eyes and

said," I just wanted to see if I could do it." He

turned around and went into the church and laid

back down in the casket. I was freaked out when

I got to the service and he had the same exact

outfit on in my dreams.

Suicide is a selfish and coward way of

getting attention. For as many people you think

don't like you, there are three that love you, look

around without the self-pity eyes. Family and

friends know the warning signs of suicide and

help save a life. Life may be short, but it is

precious. No matter what your mind thinks or

what anyone says to you. Nothing is that bad to

end your life with all the people God put into it,

so you would not feel that way. Wake up people.

Love life. It belongs to you and you deserves to

live and strive for happiness. Never get tired of life.

So, I say to you again. What does death mean to you?

To some death means:
CRYING IN SILENCE

No, I'm not weak

I just need to speak

Listen without judgmental eyes

It's Ok we all sometimes have to cry

But I'm strong and I can't show weakness

So I go over here in the corner and cry in silence

Naw I'm good is the lie I will tell you

After wiping away my tears you don't notice

Go on with your life and your problems

Your superman will always be here

Yes, I'm strong but I'm human too And with

the duty of never letting anyone down

Why do you not understand that my soul is

weak?

And my knees are buckling.

But don't worry I'll just cry in silence

Because me crying will make me weak to

you.

SUICIDE PREVENTION HOTLINE.ORG

1-800-273-8255

Lord should I grieve because

the rose bush has thorns. Or rejoice because the

thorn bush has roses?

-Unknown-

SURVIVAL

My life after shooting the ex-boyfriend

took a turn, which I most definitely didn't see

coming. I remember watching Oprah Winfrey

one day and the topic was about rape victims

and how to deal with a situation if it happens to

you. They talked about how the rapist loves

control and fighting them is what makes them continue with the rape. They also discuss the power that these sick rapists may have over you from the fear of them and what they are doing to you. If it was not for Oprah I might not have been here to tell you this part of my life.

Thank you, Oprah.

Me and the kids were bored so we decided to catch the bus to the south side and hang out with my friend L.A and her kids. The bus stop was about two blocks from her house. As we were walking down the block a car pulled up and asked where I was going. When I saw who it was. I couldn't remember his name, but I knew his face. He gave us a ride to L.A house and then kind of invited himself by offering to buy pizza and beer. We played spades and hung out till around nine. I had missed the last bus and really wanted to go home instead of spending the night at my sister

Punkin house. He offered me a ride home and I

said "Thanks". By the time we arrived at my

house, the kids were fast asleep. So, when he

offered to help me carry the kids in, I didn't think

anything of it. After the kids were in the house, I

began to carry them one by one to bed. When I put

the last kid to bed I went back down stairs and we

sat and talked for about an hour. I excused myself

to go to the bathroom. When I opened the door, he

was standing in front of it and tried to kiss me. I

pushed him away and told him I was cool I'm

single for a reason. He pulled me closer and then

barged me into my bedroom. I began to get scared

and started struggling with him, but he had

managed to get me on my bed and pulled down

my jogging pants. I started kicking at him, but he

just got stronger and began to start choking me. As

I was gasping for air all I could think about was how I was going to die, and my kids are going to find me in my bed with my cloths halfway off, dead. Before I could let a tear roll down my face I thought about what I saw on

Oprah and then I just laid there motionless. About a few minutes later he had the nerve to ask me if I wanted him to stop.

When I said, 'Yes'. He replied "No you don't ". Then he began to hump harder. I stood my ground and remained motionless. I tried to put my mind in another place to help the pain, by then he stops. He pulled up his pants and left. It worked he lost interest and didn't even had a chance to ejaculate. I ran to my door and locked it.

I then ran upstairs and checked on the kids. Once I saw they were ok. I jumped in the shower to wash his filth off me and I cried. The biggest mistake that I learned that I made was from watching a lot of Law and Order. Was not going to the emergency room and maybe save the next person he may rape. Once I got out the shower and put on clean fresh cloths. I took the cloths I had on and threw them in the trash. I sat down on the couch and tried to wrap my mind around what happened. There was a knock at the door. I was scared that he came back to finish me off. I grabbed a butcher knife and ask who was knocking at my door. It was my neighbor Nisha. When she walked in she jumped down my throat about having this guy at my house. Then she began to tell me that he has HIV and was going around giving it to whoever because he was mad that some woman gave it to him. My mouth drops, and I just busted into tears. I explained to her what had happened and then I asked her to watch the kids while I go to the E.R. I got tested and was upset because I could not describe him or give the police officers a real name to save my life, my mind was so boggled. I felt so dirty and worthless. I'm 23 and was by no means ready to die especially not from HIV. That's when I really began to have a grudge against men. Nisha and L.A was my biggest support system after the attack. They never let me be home alone and showed me so much love. I thank them very dearly for that. When I got my results back, the doctor told me that the fact of him not ejaculating inside me may have save my life. The test was negative, and I have been tested every year after that. Again, Thank You Oprah!   It took about a year and a half and months of counseling for me to be comfortable enough to even let anyone touch me again. The depression and worries had me in a place that I thought I may never be able to come out of. Yet the thought of being a lesbian was beginning to look even more of a great option around this time for real. I decided that before I go completely gay I would give men one last chance. That's when Clayton came into the picture. Clayton wasn't your average guy he was 6 foot something, light skin with a sexy body and a wonderful smile. He was a guy who loved the streets, but he was a man who was full of fun. He also was very out spoken and not afraid of anything. Our chemistry was great, and we cared so much about each other. Clayton was my best friend and lover. I did not feel right having sex with him without telling him about my attack a year and a half before him. I was unable to hold back the tears as I told the story. Clayton held and comforts me in a way that I have never felt from a man before. He made me feel safe and like a human being again.

We were never officially a couple, but it was hard to tell people that because we were around each other so much. The day that made me truly fall in love with him was when he came over to chill and we were listening to 103 Jams. They were playing all the good but oldies that afternoon. Well the music did something to us because the passion within us rose. When Guy Piece of My Love came on the radio. We made love. Now I have made love to past lovers before but never had anyone make love to me like that. If I could had picked any man in the world back then to be my soul mate, lover and friend. I would have chosen Clayton every time

He really impressed me one day when my son walked in on us having sex. My son was furious and began to fight Clayton. He let my oldest son get a few punches in and then he held him until he calmed down and had a talk with him. I do not know what he said to him, but my son was calm and went back to bed. After a few months I wanted more out of what we had but Clayton wasn't ready to settle down. So, we continued what we had until he got arrested. I never saw Clayton again.

Well five years later I did see Clayton one day on the bus and when I told him I was gay he was so mad at me. We had a small heated discussion on the bus, and then when his stop came up he left with the look of disappointment all on his face. Clayton is the only person in this world that I would apologize to for being a lesbian. Years later I was able to get in contact with Clayton and tell him I'm sorry and how I felt then. He had no idea how deep it was with me and now he is happily engaged. Do I regret anything? Hell, no I wish him the best and hope that we can remain friends. I guess you can say life is what you make of it after all the bad things have come and gone.   After Clayton I lost my freaking mind. I did a complete 360 and forgot all about men and began my journey with the same sex.

Some many years later I did meet another man at my sister Punkin's house that caught my interest and this man is tall, brown and handsome. He has a smile you can just melt for and it was something about this man name RaShan Bell. I do not have to see him, and I could feel when he come into a room. This man brought the woman out of me that no man has ever been able to do. When Shan is around me I turn straight into a female with him. I be acting all cute and cross my leg and even get a soft tone to my voice with him. It used to drive me crazy because I never encountered anything like this with a man. I had to see if maybe he is the man to make me wants to be heterosexual instead of homosexual. He did try to have a relationship with me, but I was not ready for what he was ready for in a relationship plus I was waiting for

L.A to come home and I wanted to be with her not him, so we just remain friends.

You are just a sum total of all your life experiences.

-D.L Hughley-

360 DEGREES

I called up one of my homeboys I use to
buy weed from and did some extra leg work for
to hook me up with a cute girl.

Two days later I get a call from her and we

chatted on the phone for about three days before

she told me to meet her at her mother house, so

we can put a face behind the voice. When I

arrived I really didn't know what to expect when

she come out. She may be dirt ball ugly. When

she came outside I was surprised to see she was

beautiful and had all the things I liked. A nice

booty, big boobs, a smile and spunk. We hit it off

good and the first time we slept together we

shared those three words. I love you.

It was perfect, I worked and did the husband thing

and she stayed at home and did the wife thing. My

kids did not care for her much at first, but she

helped me raised my kids as if they were her own.

We had so much fun together and for once

in my life I was happy. Like all couples there was

some up and down periods, but we managed to

work them out and stay together. Sweetest Day

came around and I asked her to marry me. Her

saying yes made me take life a little more

seriously. I began to save money for a bigger

house and a better car than the 87 Chevy Caprice

Classic I had. Once we moved out the projects things began to change and so did we.

We all make the mistake of thinking that working hard and giving your family one night a week is enough. Your spouse and children require much more attention than that alone. I found out the hard way. She began to cheat on me and then the fistfighting started. I was so hurt that I did what she did and cheated too. She never expected or had one thought of me doing that to her. I guess it woke her up because she called it truths and we decided to start over again. That's when I took her by her hand and escorted her to the front porch and told her "Hi my name is Rainy, what's yours". She says," Tisha." And that she thinks my name was so cute and sweet.   I had gotten me another job that pays more money. That's when I bought her a car, taught her how to drive and kept her happy any way I could. I guess that and all the sex we were having wasn't enough because she became lonely. One day I wasn't feeling too well and was lying down in the bed. She comes into the room and asks if she could have this friend over whom she just meet off the street. She began to tell me how nice and sweet this guy is and how she wants me to meet him. I really wasn't feeling it and sure didn't want to meet some young ass thug. So, I told her no, but it was too late she already had him sitting downstairs. When I went downstairs and saw this dude I knew it was going to be a lot of trouble and drama. It was something about him that didn't sit well with me. When he left I told her that he looks like a woman beater and she should just leave him alone. I told her she may get hurt. Also, it's not like we need extra drama in our lives. I was

already fed up with all her anger and jealously

issues plus we fist fought way too much. Having

this guy come over was the last straw, so

I started sleeping in the spare room.

I say about a week later my nephew and

me were out riding around and smoking, when I

had the strangest feeling

That someone was in my house that shouldn't

be. So, we headed back home. On the way God

warned me with signs that something was not

right. The first sign was when I saw someone in

the store that looked just like this boy. The

second was a billboard with the bible scripture

Luke 8:17. For nothing is secret, that shall not be

manifest; neither anything hid, that shall not be

known and come abroad. In other words:

What's done in the dark will come to light.

When I saw that I told my nephew that there's

going to be trouble when we get home so brace

yourself.

We pulled up and you can hear people

running around the house hard. I opened the door

and then everything was quiet. I yelled for everyone

to get the hell out my house. Then Tisha, this boy and

her friends came running out of the attic. I grabbed

her by her arm and we began to argue.

This boy told her that she can come stay with

him and that she doesn't have to put up with

me anymore.

When she told him no she is staying here, she loves

me. This boy handed his friend his nine-millimeter

and just out of nowhere beat her up like none of us

was there. I felt bad at first until he started yelling,

"Be careful who you tell you love. My heart is

nothing to play with". He grabbed his gun and left.

I helped her up and told her that is what she gets.

By then he returned and apologizes for

disrespecting my home. He then told me how he

loves her and that she told him the same thing and

how unhappy she was with me. He turned to her

and said he will be waiting outside for her. Next

thing you know she ran upstairs grabbed her gun and started shooting at him out the bedroom window. I took the gun from her and threw her out my house. She was so lucky my kids weren't there, or she would have gotten two ass whipping that night.

She continued to try to come see me and get back together every chance she got. I told her no, but I won't stop her from seeing the kids. We had been together for two years at that time.

One day she comes to get the kids to take them to the park. Later on, I find out that she shot at this boy again with my kids in the car. I goes to the boy house to get my kids and as I was gathering them. His friend had a red beam on my head. The boy stood in front of me and said that he won't let his friend shoot me and that it's all about her and what she wants. He told her to choose between me and him. She said him. I told them to have a nice life. I just want my kids and to stay away from us and live they life together, then I left.

She came over a couple of nights later crying about how he is still sleeping with his baby momma and she only picked him because he told her he would kill me if she didn't.

They were together for about a year and when he got arrested for shooting his baby momma in the stomach with a 12 gauge, here she come and like a fool I took her back.

We were together for another three years, but we just could not stop the arguing and fighting. So, we split up. Till this day we are still friends and talk to each other on the phone. If I could sum up our relationship, I would say it was the worst and best relationship I ever had at the same time. I dated a few more women after her and really began to

explore the lesbian lifestyle. A lifestyle that I have

grown to love.

Do love finds you or do you find love, or is

love just your lust, for the desires for which you

think you love?

~RainyRain~

CELL BLOCK

When I finally told my family I was gay, the biggest support I got was from my big sister Gerl, my Aunt Pookie and all my nieces and nephews.

Everyone else had they say about me and how my kids weren't being raised right and all that bull shit. It hurt me that people think because you're gay that you're a child molester or doesn't know how to do things because you're gay. Oh, my all the myths. Being a homosexual is a very emotional and physical thing that most people do not understand. In my journey I have witness racism, attempted rape, actual rape and so much ridicule from Christians and non-Christians alike because I made the conscience decision to love a woman open and freely. Let me set one thing straight with everyone. When we close our eyes, we see what you see. When you bleed we bleed. We are all humans. The only thing that separates us is the ignorance you show within yourselves. I may be gay, but I am a mother and a child of God first and foremost.   This part of my life is when I had a serious wake up call. I knew I was wrong but when it comes to your kids I guess there is no wrong.   People started smiling in my face and stabbing me in my back. Nothing new to that one. I had $700 in food stamps and one pack of chicken in my freezer. My welfare case

worker messed up my case, so I had got it late

plus some. When I came out of the closet.

People suddenly too busy to take gas money.

My homeboy came by with a friend who had

a car. I asked him to take me to the grocery

store. He told me I had to drive myself, but I

had to wait till he makes a run for his mom.

They came back and when I got in the car I see

the steering wheel peeled and tied with a blue

bandana. He tried to tell me that he lost his key

and was late for work, so he peeled his own car.

"Whatever. All I want is to get my kids some

groceries before they get home from school. " I

go get the groceries, come back to the house,

they left. After I put the groceries up, I noticed I

forgot the flour to fry the chicken. On my way

back to the store, I had to pee. I stopped at my

aunt Pookie house to use the bathroom and she tells me how they cut her food stamps down to $16. That's ridiculous. I get a shopping list from her, so I can get her some extra groceries. I get the groceries and headed back to my aunt house. That's when the state troopers pulled me over because the windshield was cracked. I was on the borderline of one county to the next and since the car was stolen. To the next county I was 30 miles away.

Out of all the dumb shit I have done and could have went to jail for I get locks up over this. I called every number I could think of and everyone had a block on their phone. I knew my best friend who had moved to Texas by this time would answer the phone. But I couldn't remember her number to save my life. The first three days of jail, I cried and all I could think about was my children. The correction

officer came to my pod and handed me an

envelope. It was papers from children services

saying they have my kids. I finally remembered

my best friend number in Texas then I called

her to get in touch with my family to let them

know where I was at. I got sent to the hole for

two days for rampaging and tearing up my cell

after that. I felt like I have died and gone to

hell. Rumor has it that I left my children there

by themselves to visit a girl I was dating in PA.

She did use to come get me every weekend, but

I had my kids with me every time.

My oldest son got him, his sister and

brother ready for school. He also cooked for

them for two days before they told anyone I

never came home.   A few weeks later I go to

court and it turned out that the stolen car was a

Minister of a church Mr. Clarence Glenn. I have never felt so ashamed in my life. He wrote me a letter saying how he forgive me and to get my life together. I spent three months in jail and my case worker would bring the kids once a week to see me. The first time they came. I cried because they had to see me through a glass and they cried because I was behind that glass. It was the hardest thing I had to deal with in my life to see how disappointed my kids were of me. I am the one who was supposed to be there to protect them.

While I was locked up I did what most jail mates do. I adapted to my surroundings, exercised like crazy, played dominoes, went to classes, church, gave massages for commissary and called on God. Funny how we only call on him during a crisis. I met some interesting people in jail and learned some new and weird things. I learned to put a feminine pad in my shoes for comfort, roll up toilet paper for a Q-tip and make wine out of fruit cocktail and bread. You learn to be very creative in jail with a lot of time on your hands.

Now don't get me wrong jail is no place to be. The feeling of hopelessness will have you going crazy. Especially with all those spirits coming in and out. You must eat and sleep when they tell you to. It's colder than Alaska and all you get is one blanket, a pair of shoes that don't fit and one uniform. I used to hide blankets and extra cloths in my bed. Oh, let's not forget the main thing missing your FAMILY. The biggest lesson is learning who has your back and who doesn't. Other than my kids I got one letter from my girlfriend at that time, but it was only after I

sent her these two

poems…

IT'S COOL

It's cool how you don't write me
It's cool how you don't care

It's cool how the words I Love You are just

floating in the air

We all make mistakes, you do

too   I'll never say those words,

when my actions means fuck you

Sit back and think of who's hurting who

Hang on to my cloths I still want to
confront you   I hope everything is well with
your health and all

Even though I'm mad I still don't want to see
you

fall

Take care of yourself and don't forget about
school

I know the next time I won't be anyone's fool

It's cool how you don't write me

It's cool how you don't care
It's cool how the words I Love You

Are just floating in the air

IT'S COOL

HOW COME YOU DON'T WRITE ME

When you know you can't call

How come I write you and you don't respond
at all

It don't take a genius to get some paper and
a pen Unless you don't want to know how
the hell I've been

You just take my heart and cut it with a
knife

I bet you wouldn't be doing me this way if you
made me

a part of your life

But I'm not and it's cool I guess it's time for a new start

I'm tired of saying this and I'm tired of you breaking my

heart!

BROKEN HEARTS BLEED TOO!

After getting some of my anger out the way I wanted to and trying to figure out why this is happening to me I wrote this.

THANK YOU, LORD

Thank You Lord

For my sons and daughter

These blessings you gave me is where I get my joy from

Thank You Lord

For the life you given me

For without you I cannot be free

Thank You Lord

For opening my eyes

For I know you're the only God in the
skies

Thank You Lord

For letting me live

For it is your choice for me to continue to
live

You have chosen me out of so many

To show how your love alone is plenty

So I

Thank You Lord

And

Thank You again

For showing me that you ARE my one and
only True

Friend.

Now one of the inmates wrote this and I

thought it was beautiful.

As my mind wonders

My soul fades watching
You alone in the shade

Uncluttered by sensation
I see you stand up and walk down the sidewalk

I long to hold you

Caress you

Walk with you

Simply talk to you

I long for the day you turn and walk with me
But for now

I'll continue to dream!

I learned a lot about myself and the life I

want me and my children to have. I came up

with a game plan and got a lot of help from

classes that give us flyers like this:

<u>AS</u> <u>A</u> <u>PERSON</u> <u>YOU</u> <u>HAVE</u> <u>THE</u> <u>RIGHT</u> <u>TO</u> BE TREATED WITH RESPECT

BE LISTEN TO AND TAKEN
SERIOUSLY

SET YOUR OWN PRIORITES

SAY NO WITHOUT FEELING GUILTY

CHANGE YOUR MIND

HAVE YOUR NEEDS BE AS IMPORTANT
AS THE

NEEDS OF OTHERS

GROW, LEARN AND CHANGE

FEEL AND EXPRESS ANGER

BE YOURSELF

CHOOSE NOT TO ASSERT YOURSELF

ASSERTIVE BAHAVIOR- STANDING UP
FOR

WHAT I THINK AND FEEL WHILE RESPECTING

THE RIGHTS OF OTHERS.

MOVING FORWARD

When I got released I was on five years of

probation, restitution fees and weekly

visitations with my kids. Once I arrived at my

home I knew the utilities would be off but when I opened my front door. It was emptied. Everything kid's toys, cloths, furniture and including my period panties were gone. Someone has cleaned me completely out. It was two days before Thanksgiving. I cried myself to sleep.

The next day, I went to my sister Punkin house to get my mail. When I got there, she snuck up behind me and threw me up against the wall and patted me down for weapons. I was a little confused, but I remembered that when I found out that she was behind my kids being in foster homes, I wrote her a very angry and threatening letter from jail. If it was not for my little nephew Andre being there yeah, I would have burned her precious house to the ground.

I know that is what she loves more than anything. I felt like if my kids did not have nowhere to stay she shouldn't nether. I told her my focus is getting my kids back and leaving Youngstown. I was far past my anger and I know revenge is not mines it's his and so I left her in God hands.

I did everything my probation officer and CPS case worker told and asked me to do. I attended rehab and parenting meetings, found a job and kept all my visitation appointments. I missed my kids so much and when Christmas came around I still put up my tree and surrounded it with presents. I know it would not make up for what I did to them by my actions, but I had to let them know in every way that I was sorry and love them.

I was able to see them at

the house a day before

Christmas and give them

one gift from me to open.

It meant so much to them.

When Valentines' Day came around I

had finished my classes. I always got my kids

something for that day to let them know that

they were my Valentine. Just because we were

apart I did not want to leave them hanging so I

had my friend Tori deliver they gifts to their

schools. My caseworker Jason fussed at me for

doing it because it was against my terms and I

was only allowed supervised visits. When I

apologized and told him that if I wanted to

kidnap my kids I would have done it already

because I found out where they were living and

when I gave him addresses his mouth dropped.

My oldest just so happened to be with a lady I somewhat met a year prior at The Tom Joyner Morning Show when they came to Powers

Auditorium. She won first place in the old school dance contest and my baby boy Eric won second. My daughter happened to be with her cousin on her father side and Eric was with my best friend L.A fathers' girlfriend and I got to sneak and see him more when he would be over his house. God do work in mysterious ways, doesn't he?

Five long months pasted before I was done with all they asked of me and my kids were returned to me two days before my birthday. I invited all my nieces and nephews to bring they kids and had a welcome home party for them. I slept with all three in my bed for about a week and it still seemed like I could not hold, hug and kiss them enough.

We became much closer after that and we always kept each other in our eyesight. I was so happy yet sad at the same time. I wanted more for my kids and myself. Every time you turned around someone was getting killed and they were dying younger and younger. With my boys approaching their teens, my oldest son Dominique started having trouble in school himself with the badgering of me being gay and the pressure of joining a gang. One day Dominique was walking up the street and I was in the house when Eric came running in yelling that Dominique's bleeding. Now the first thought was that someone had shot my baby. I ran out the house and jumped over the banister and ran towards him. He was beat up pretty

bad. I was furious I called the police and made a

report, but it was not enough, but I had to do

the adult thing right? Well I just had enough

and let that incident get the best of me and I

called one of my little cousins

Glen to come help my son fight these boys, so

it'll be one on one. Five minutes later I got

about fifteen kids walking to my house trying

to beat up two boys. Next thing I knew the cops

were coming up the street, I had all the kids

hide in the house and made the police report

outside. That's when the adult kicked in and I

told the kids to let go of it and tried to talk some

sense into them and then I gave them all some

money to go to the store with the warning that

no one better not be stealing shit from any store.

Just when I thought it was all over again here

comes a kid yelling, telling me that they all are fighting around the corner. When I get around the corner my son and his cousin are beat up on the boys but this time the boys got two other boys. By the time I broke some of them up I saw one of the kids had a knife I told him to get back to my house now and broke the fight up. Someone had called the cops and a lot of the kids ran. After stuff dyed down a little I took my cousin and his friends' home. Later that night after the kids was in bed I realized that I had too much power and that this is not what I want for us I started crying and praying for relief from it all this environment, my lust for women, everything. I even prayed for a husband. No matter what I knew I needed to get away from here bad I was too worried and afraid for our lives. I knew that if we stayed in

Youngstown that things would not get better for us. So, I planned and plotted to get out by any means necessary and fast. Ann has been trying for a couple of years to get me and the kids to come to Texas. So, I made that call and started to prepare to move to Killeen, Texas. When the kids went to school I hit the streets and sold almost everything. Weed, crack, pills, cigarettes and cigars.

You name it if I can sell it I did. I was living three lives. Drug dealer in the day, mom in the evening and lesbian at night because I was still sleeping with women thru all this. My kids had no clue of what was going on actually. I always tried to hide a lot from them and let them know what they needed to know. I packed up three big bags. One had our cloths, one had electronics and the other had dry goods plus we each had a book bag. A few days before my

daughters fifth birthday we got on the

Greyhound and took a two-and-a-half-day ride

to Killeen, Texas.

    THEY SAY PEOPLE CAN'T CONTROL YOUR

HAPPINESS

BUT THEY SURE DO HAVE A LOT TO DO WITH

YOUR SADNESS!!!   ~RainyRain~

L.A

No this is not a chapter about Los Angeles, California.

No not at all. In a lot of the earlier chapters I mention L.A, well now I am going to tell you more about me and Laticia Alexander in this chapter.

First off I wish I could tell you how we really met, but we both could not tell you if we tried. I just know that I have been knowing L.A since we were fifteen years old. We never had any classes together. We just used to always run into each other plus she used to stay with my cousin Pooh. She was adopted, and her adopted parents use to hang out with my Uncle Nate back in the day.

Me and Tish were both some odd kids in school. People use to pick on us and we use to get into some fights we didn't want to get into. I stopped seeing her so much when she left South

High School to go to The

Rayen

High School.

We lost touch for a long while, even after

I graduated from high school, we lost touch.

One day I went to a going away party for one of

my brothers in

Christ who was going off into the Air force Billy

Hendrix. I was enjoying myself and talking to

someone when I hear "Lorraine McQueen,

Bitch where the hell you been?"

I turn around and it's Tish. We yelled, screamed

and hugged for a long time, tell each other how

we miss each other. After our lengthy hug, I

noticed she was pushing a stroller with the

most gorgeous, chunky little boy I have seen.

"Who pretty ass baby you stole?"

"Mines, his name is Samarr."

"Oh my God he is too cute. You know I'm gonna steal

him, right?"

"Girl bye, you are not gonna steal my baby."

"Shiiit. Watch me."

"Rainy, I don't have time for you, I just know you are

not getting my baby."

"OK, whatever Tish."

We laugh and continue to enjoy the party.

When it was time to leave, Tish asked me was I

driving, and could she get a ride home. Of

course, I took her home. Once we got to her

house, she realized that she locked her key in

the house and her roommate went out of town

for the night.

"Well what you gonna do I looked around the

whole house and saw no way to get in. You and

the baby are more than welcome to chill with me at my house till she comes back. Plus, my daughter loves babies, so he will be just fine and will have someone to play with him."

"You sure I do not want to be a burden?"

"Girl get in the damn car." Her roommate called about three in the morning checking on her since she was not at the house. When she told her where she was at her roommate said she would come pick her and the baby up. "Um. Don't know what you think this is, but you will not take this baby out the house at this time or he will get sick. I'll bring him home in the morning."

"What? I can't take my baby home?"

"Nope. You know I'm old school and it's too late to be taking a two-month-old baby out in that air. See ya in the morning bye."

"Ain't this about a bitch? You serious too?"

"You know it. You know he's safe."

"Whatever Rainy I better have my baby at my house

when you get up."

"Yes Ma'am."

When I took him home a week later he had

clothes, diapers, milk, etc.

"You ain't shit! You know I don't have a car to

come get my baby and you such a busy body. I

never know if you are home. Got me worried.'

"Shut the hell up. How you worried when you

talked to him every day after you cusses me

out. Shut up!

Help

me get all his stuff out the car."

"What stuff?"

"Um he only had a change of clothes and a diaper bag.

So now he set for about two months."

"You make me sick."

"Love you too."

"You didn't have to do all this. You could've

just brought my baby the fuck home.'

"Yeah, yeah but love at first sight and you

already told me about his punk ass sperm

donor and I know him personally and how he

is. So, guess what? Luke I am his Father."

After that I went to Tish house every morning

after I got my kids off to school with some

McDonald's and two blunts. We got

reacquainted with each other and caught up on

lost times.

One day we were chillin and me and the kids

was spending the night over with her and hers.

She had four kids at this time. We started talking about people we use to have a crush on in high school and by my surprise she gonna tell me a whole story and when I asked who it was. She says "You."

 And then ran upstairs and locked herself in her bedroom.

I was stuck. I didn't see that coming and I liked her too but never said anything. From that point on I was trying to get with Tish hard, but she would tell me No every fucking time.

She never let the fact that we liked each other stand in the way of our friendship and even though at the time I hated it. I respected it the same. Our friendship had some trying times and man did we go through some stuff. If it is ringing a bell to you I mention L.A in a few of the earlier chapters. The beginning of our tough times to me was when we were helping her mom with some food for a church Bar B Que because her parents were Evangelist and deacon of a church. I will never forget the ribs was about done and me and Ma was talking, and she was telling me of how much of a good friend I was to Tish and how she wished she had more friends like me. She also told me to look after her and always be by her side. I thought it was a little weird that after all this time we have spent together why Ma telling me this now. I paid it no mind. Once the ribs were done. Me and Tish started taking the pans of meat in the house when Ma collapses and falls down two to three steps. I had just put my pan down and grabbed Tish's when we heard her Yell. We ran outside to see her laying on the ground.

"Ma! What happened? Can you talk?"

"Yeah baby, I'm OK just got a little dizzy. Where's my wig? Is my wig still on my head?"

Tish says, "Really Momma you are lying on the ground can't move and you worried about a wig." "Wow. Ma, we don't care about that wig. Can you move your legs and arms? Do you feel any pain?"

"I don't feel my legs."

Me and Tish look at each other with concern.

Ma was in pretty bad shape to where they had to amputate both legs. When Ma was in the hospital. I went to make a run and I rolled me a blunt and was just driving, deep into thought. I dazed off and when I came out of my daze I was in front of Tish house. I thought to myself how the hell I ended up here. I parked my car and went into the house. Tish was sitting upstairs crying.

"What's wrong Boo why are you crying?'

"Mom gone Rainy, my momma gone. She's dead."

"What the hell!"

I just broke down and we held each other and cried. For some reason I could not get myself to go to the funeral plus I had to work so the night before I went to the funeral home to pay my respects and when I entered the door and saw Ma laying there I froze. I couldn't move. It seemed like the more I tried to walk toward her the more I didn't move. I just stared at her from the door and cried. After watching a few people go in and pay their respect. I realize that I am not going any further in there, I turned around, signed the book and sat in my car in the parking lot. All I could do was think of why I just could not get myself to go kiss the woman I consider like a Mom to me. The only thing I

could come up with was the guilt of her last

conversation to me and how deep down I

wanted her daughter to be more than a friend.

After that and some time has passed, I moved to

Texas. I was still on probation and had to come
back to

Ohio to see my probation officer. I stopped by

to see Tish and the kids and once I saw Samarr

and how chunky and big he got I wanted to

bring him to Texas with me.

I notice that Tish had this look on her face like

she was in danger or someone is after her. I

kept asking her what was wrong, and she says

nothing. I could not shake the feeling that

something was wrong with my friend. I told her

that I have to come back in a month and a half

and that I will get Samarr for the summer. She

was relucted, but she said OK and then I left to

get back on the Greyhound for Texas.

Before that month was up, Tish sister

Keishma calls me to tell me she is in prison for

robbery and murder. I hurried and checked the

local news website to see that it was true, my

best friend was locked up. I did everything I

could to get Samarr, but because I was not

blood related and lived in another state, my

money did not matter. I could not get the one I

truly considered a son. It broke my heart.

Tish did not murder anyone she just was with

the wrong people and let the trials of society,

peer pressure and desperateness cause her to be

involved in a robbery where a man was killed.

Tish got seven years prison time and five years

of probation. The others involved got 25 to life.

While she was away I did all I could to stay in contact with the kids, especially Samarr.

Me and Tish wrote every week. After about a year she finally gave me a chance at being in a relationship together. Yes, I finally got her. Prison will let you see who is true and who is not. I used to send her money every other month and a lump sum every income tax. Our letters were funny to nasty. We had a great communication ship. We even had our arguments through letters. One day, she wrote me and tried to break up. She wanted me to live my life and not wait on her, no matter how much I told her that I was content with waiting on her. She wouldn't have it we argued in letters for a month before I said fine and started fucking other people. That's how I even got

things started with Shun.

The whole time she is in jail and I am writing

her, I did have some issues in my relationships

for writing her. They were insecure about a

woman that was thousands of miles away

locked up in a prison, never understood

that.
By Tish sixth year in prison, I decided to go

back to Ohio. When I left my daughter was five

and she could not remember who my sisters or

her cousins were. I felt it was time for her to see

where she was from. So, we packed up for a

two-week vacation and drove to

Ohio. On the way we stopped at the prison and

visited Tish for the first time. I was so nervous. I

hadn't seen my friend and woman in eight

years.

When we got there, it was crazy cause everyone in there knew who I was and was excited to see me like they were her. She talked about me and our relationship so much to the women there and they loved the relationship we had and the loyalty I had for her. Seeing her was exciting to see my skinny Tish all thick and looking good, like prison did something good to her. Due to me being from out of town we were able to have two visits in the same day. We had a blast, ate lunch and took pictures.

When our two weeks was up, and it was time to go, I went to start my car and it would not start. My sister Punkin knew someone that could come to the house and fix it. My starter had gone out and it was like the man had x-ray vision because every bit of the money I had left to get back home down to the penny is what it costed me to get it fix.

I figured that since we still have a few weeks before school start I could get a job real fast and take the first check to get back home. Yeah right, forgot I have a felony and could not get a job till four months later.

So, me and Lil Rain stayed in Ohio.

Tish had a year left so I figured why not see where it goes and then we can go back to Texas together. Every Sunday I would go to her dad house and clean up and cook for him and help him get clothes ready for church the next week and we would watch football and Duck Dynasty. Also, every Sunday Tish would call, and we would talk for two phone calls. Dad started getting jealous. He said she didn't call

this much till I got there.

By the time Tish was released I had a

two=bedroom house, clothes, shoes and all she

would need home waiting on her. She was

released to her dad address and me, my

daughter and her father got her a bed and he

helped me put it together for her, I even got her

a TV for her room.

A few days after her release we went to

Mill Creek Park and had our own private

commitment of vows. We had a beautiful

marriage and family. Our love for each other

showed everywhere we go. People was always

telling us how they can't wait to have a love

and relationship like ours. Even our kids

admired what we had and how we were with

each other. Everything was going great until

one day out of nowhere. Tish accused me of cheating on her. Now if you ask me I say she got the bull shit from my punk ass cousin who wanted my woman, son and life. She wanted to be me and wanted to see my family fall apart. Now this is not the first time Tish was acting so different and strange to me for a while now. She started shutting me out, neglecting me physically and we seemed to always bicker about something. I loved her so much that I myself was on an emotional roller coaster right along with her.

When a person has been institutionalized for a long period of time, when they are released it is a huge shock to the brain due to the change in time, technology and the severity of how easy it is to get locked back up. At the time I had no idea or understanding that she left having a best friend and five elementary

age children and had to come home to a fiancée,

two adults and three teenagers. So much was

missing out of her life to her, along with all the

nightmares and insecurities, our marriage was

falling.   I was in Paramedic school and I was

close to taking my finals. With all that was

going on at home I was struggling to pass my

exams. I was also working 8 – 10 hour shifts at

the nursing home. One day I was getting ready

for school and I woke Tish up, so she can get

ready for work. She was dragging talking about

she doesn't feel like going. I wake her anyway,

and tell her to get up and go to work. I

proceeded downstairs to finish cooking

breakfast. When I come back to the room she is

sitting on the end of the bed shaking her head

talking about how her Dad is going to be upset with her.

When I asked why, she said because she quit her job.

My mouth dropped. Now in my head I was thinking….

"Bitch you worried about your dad who lives in California and we're struggling and got three teenagers who about to graduate and you worried about him." I lost it. I quietly went downstairs ate my breakfast wrote her a letter telling her that if I am going to do it by myself, I might as well be by myself. I taped my wedding band to the letter, stuck it in her car and left for school. That was the worst thing I ever could have done. Samarr found the letter instead. My bond with our son has been dented ever since. I moved out a month later and all me and Tish did for a whole year was play the blame game, dated people to make each other jealous, work out some problems but not all and fucked. We both were an emotional wreck and our divorce was taking a hold of not just us but the kids as well.

We had finally got to the point that we need to stay away from each other for a while and clear our heads. So, we tried to keep away from each other it lasted for about a week until late one night, November 7, 2015 to be exact, I get rudely awaken by my daughter because my first great nephew Ty-Shawn got hit by a car while walking home and was in bad shape. In the hospital after I got what little information I could get, I began to pray, as I got done saying my prayer, I lifted my head and behold Tish is walking towards me.

She hugs me and says,

"No matter what water head, I'll continue being mad at you after all this is over." After finally getting to go back and see my nephew like that I knew he was not coming home and I couldn't take it I needed some air. After about an hour we see that my nephew must have more tests done. I told my niece that I will bring her a shot of liquor, a pillow and blanket, and that I will be back.

Me and Tish rode to my house so I can get away and grab the stuff for my niece. When we got in the car she hands me a blunt and says,

> "I don't smoke but I got a blunt just for you I know you need it right now."

My best friend who was in town to bury her father a few days prior, called me and said she left her wallet in my car. So, after we get the stuff from my house and get to my best friend house, I gave her the wallet, let her know what was going on and I turned around to head back towards the car. As I was walking to the car I see Tish going crazy and crying. Now on the ride from my house to drop off the wallet we got a call that her dad was rushed to the hospital in California. When I got to the car Tish Dad is dead. It happened that fast. We both on the phone with a kid and we all meet at my house to grieve. Soon after we tell all the kids about they grandfather, my phone rings, my nephew has an hour left to live. WHAT THE FUCK! I KNOW RIGHT!

I wish I could make this up.

No matter how angry, hurt, upset and disappointed in each other we were, none of that mattered now. I needed her, and she needed me. I had always been the strong one with my friends and family, so I was planning two funerals, running between two families and dealing with a sour divorce. I was so numb. The only release that worked was all the sympathy sex me and Tish was having with each other. We got each other through the grief till about the beginning of the next year then all that we were fighting about suddenly surfaced again. Tish wanted to get back together but I felt that she wasn't ready yet. Me spoiling Tish and making sure everything is done was enabling her and making it hard for her to be the wife I knew she could be for me. I knew I had to stand my ground or we would be back in that emotional roller coaster that got us divorced in the first place. During all this the yearning and calling to go back to Texas was growing stronger each day. I tried getting Tish to just stay separated till she gets off probation and then she can move to Texas and we continue our plans before the divorce but, this woman is a Gemini and is so fucking stubborn. If we were not together then she doesn't want nothing to do with Texas and if I left without her, she won't come back to me.

I tried sticking it out for a while but my passion for DJing and my music was calling me plus I missed my boys and grandson. So off to Texas I go.

Till this day we are good friends we never let anything get in the way of our friendship that has always came first. Yet, she is the most petty and jealous hearted woman I know when it comes to me. We will always have a special love for each other, but us being together is not in our cards anymore and over the few years she always made that clear. So we moved on.

That still does not stop the fact that the ending of the book is going to piss her the fuck off, but life must go on.

I know, I know my life and only shit like this happens to me. (Hush readers!)

I'M NOT WHO WE THINK I AM

Now this is the second trip me and my kids ever took outside of Ohio. My plans were to get to know myself and the kids better. I also wanted to reflect on my life and what it is that I wanted from Texas. My idea was for us to see and explore all the cities we get to go thru and learn to value where we are going and to get a fresh start. That didn't happen of course. The bus ride was horrible, we had to ride with a broken stall and shit smell for two stops and then we can change buses. I thought the kids was going to be a problem on the ride, especially with the boys who were 9 and 11 at the time, not really wanting to move and leave all their friends and our family. It took the kids a while to truly understand why the big sudden move.

Once we got off that bus in Killeen, Texas it was like a huge bolder fell off my back. For once in my life I felt free emotionally. I could be or deal with whoever whenever. Boy did I have plans for Texas. I really wanted to have a new start with me and the kids. I used to have a bad habit of running from my problems, but this time I was trying to run to a better solution to my old problems and that's women.

The weather was beautiful, and the scenery was pleasant. I was thinking to myself as we ride thru downtown Killen to get to Stonegate Estate,

"This is it Rain. It's now or never. Don't make this move in vain. Do better for you and these kids."   Once we got settled Ann had cooked for us and after dinner we rode around and got to see some of the nearby schools and places to go. I admit it was refreshing to not hear any gun shots. The kids seemed to be adapting well and plus we had a pool in the trailer park, along with Ann and Meko's three kids. I knew they would be glad we left and will get to learn more than what Youngstown had to offer them.   The next day I get up and was so surprised to see that I really left Ohio and was in Texas. I went outside to enjoy the Texas air and to see what the sunrise in Texas looks like. I was so overwhelmed, and breath taken by seeing the sun which looked like it was ten times bigger and brighter than I ever saw before. I felt like God sent the sun my way to tell me it will be OK. Before I knew it tears rolled down my face. I bowed my head and prayed, as I lifted my head Ann comes outside.   "Hey you up early. The time difference got you huh?"

"Naw you know I'm an early bird. I just can't believe I am here and away from all the drama. Me and the kids will actually get a chance at something."   "I know, I been told you, but you were so against coming, Now that you here I can ask why?"   "Ma said give you time with your husband and that we have to still live our separate lives. I really believe she just don't want my gayness to rub off on ya."

"Girl bye, no matter what you do, or we do for that matter is on us. We gotta answer for everything we do ain't that what she always tells us?"

"Yeah."

"Then don't let no one stop you from trying to be you. I know you be struggling with stuff and truthfully, I would love to see you with a husband like me but if a woman makes you happy then I'm happy and don't you forget it. I 'm gonna always have your back."

"Now hush and smoke." I laughed grabbed the blunt and continued to watch the sunrise. Once the blunt was done Ann was like here and handed me her car keys. I looked at her puzzled and was like. "What you are handing me keys for I don't know where or which way to go."

"Exactly! So, go get lost."
Huh."

"Go get lost it's a tank full of gas. Drive around and find your way back home."

"Are you serious?"

"Yup, Bye." Ann goes in the house and locks the door.

So, I had no choice but to get in the car and drive.

Later that night Ann took me to a club called "City Lights" It was a block or so away from where we stayed, and it was packed that Thursday night. Now let's keep in mind that one of the many reasons I left Ohio was to not be gay anymore. Yeah right, I walked right into candy land there was people of all types everywhere and I was fresh meat I had so many women come up to me trying to dance and get my number you would have thought I was a celebrity in there. It was fucking awesome. Yet I was so shy and out of place. I was polite, but I would not bite for no one. I was scared and overwhelmed. Do not get it twisted. I had a blast.   For the next few months every Thursday, Friday and Saturday I am in City Lights. I went dressed every way: like a girl, like a stud, like no body and like myself. Every time, there was always a female approaching me more than the men.

By my fifth month in Texas I was paying deposit on our first house there on upper 2nd street. I had a job at Krystal's Hamburger when I got down to Texas because Ann was working there and was about to quit so she trained me to take her spot. I was so excited to be on my own. I appreciated what Ann and Meko did for us, but I need to see if I can make it on my own here. I had a few friends that I made at Krystal's and two people who I use to talk to over the phone whenever I would call Ann from Ohio. I don't even remember where I got furniture from, but I had it all when I moved into our first house. Not long after living there, I went to the eye doctor to get some new glasses and it was this girl in there promoting a Lil Flip concert

that was coming soon. I really wasn't paying

this woman too much attention and I felt like

the Lil Flip promotion thing was a pick-up line,

so I indulged in her conversation until it was

time for me to go to the back. When I got done I

was waiting for them to call me to pick out my

frames, when I notice that this girl is still in

here, so I asked her to help me pick out some

frames. Told her I wanted a woman opinion

and that I did not want anything to girly or

manly. After picking out my frames. We went

outside to smoke a cigarette and talked some

more. She was really promoting the hell out of

Lil Flip to where I agreed to come as her guest

and I don't even like Lil Flip, my son does.

We exchanged numbers and went our way. I

calls her later that night and we talked till the sun came up. The next night I met up with her a club she used to work at as a waitress. When I walked in and saw it was a strip club I had done about lost my mind. I never saw a strip club other than on TV. I was like a kid in a candy store. My mouth dropped, I think I drooled a little.

She notices me at the door and comes to me and gives me a hug. She escorts me to a table up front but on the side of the stage and asks me what I wanted to drink. I got me a shot of Henney and a Corona. As I sit there waiting for her to come back with my drink, I enjoy the dancers on the stage. I wish I could remember her name but man! She climbs to the top of the pole did some twirls and flips then slides down the pole like a fireman on a call, but when she lands at the bottom all you heard was a thud and her in a perfect split then she shaked both butt cheeks to the song playing. Oh my God. I felt like I was on top of the world at that moment because she gets up from her position and she come over straight to me and puts her ever so soft and perfectly shaped boobs in my face and shook them softly on my cheeks. I wanted to faint. By this time, she sits on my lap and grinds on me a little and then she bite downs on my ear in a nonharmful way. My leg started shaking, she looks up at me, smile, kisses me on the cheek and got back on the stage and started collecting her money off the floor.

"Here's your drinks sorry it took so long. Are you enjoying yourself?"

"Huh? Yeah, I gotta be honest I have never been in a strip club before I'm from a small town in Ohio. "

"Oh, so than let me tell you now. I not only a waitress here I am a performer too."

"Huh? Wait! What? Say that again?" She laughs. "I'll be back. Her hold this for me." She hands me a hand full of money and disappears to back stage. Of course, I am overwhelmed with all of it and was stuck for a second. I look around put the money in my pocket and began to take my shot and drink on my beer. By the time I regrouped and got myself together then I hear coming to the stage MeMe. She does her dances, she flips, and all this money is being thrown at her. Again, my mouth wide the fuck open. So, when she gets done she picks up her money and hands it to me and exits the stage. I put the

Money in the pocket of the opposite side from

the first roll she gave me.

When the night or should I say morning

is over she asks me if I want to go get some

breakfast. I said,

"Sure."
"Cool just let me cash out and I'll meet

you at the door."

"OK. Here's your money."
"No hold on to that I got my cash out, I'll meet

you at the door." She gives me a kiss on the

cheek and walks towards the bar.

As we are walking to my car we discuss what is

open to go and get some food at.

We Decided on IHOP and it was a little

crowded, so we had to wait for about ten

minutes for a table. Once we got our table I was

a perfect gentleman and pulled out her chair for her and we sat and talk and ate and talk. I had such a good time with her that I did not want it to end. She was so friendly and pleasant, and we connected. After realizing its seven in the morning we leave IHOP and goes to my house and finish talking.

The kids were still sleep and so was my god sister Zetta who watched the kids for me while I went out. So, we quietly crept back to my room and I began to take the money she handed me out my pocket.

"How much is it?"

"I don't know it's not my money to count."

"So, you never counted how much I gave you?"

"Nope."
"Hmm. Well can you count it for me and

tell me where your rest room is?'

"Sure, it's down the hall first door on left."

"Thank you."

When I get done counting the money, why this

chick had me holding $1,278.

I couldn't help but think damn this is in one

night. That little devil on my shoulder was like,

Shit Rain you can pimp her out.

That little angel was like OK Rain you haven't

pimped since Jr. High and High School. You

came down here to do different, chill out.

So, I chilled.
When she returned to the room. I told her how

much it was. She said thanks and put the

money in her purse.

"So, you not gonna count to see if it is all
there?
You just trust everyone with your money like
that huh.

If it's like that let me get a hundred?"

"For What?"

"Aww shit, just because so I can buy me something for myself instead of the kids."

As she was going back into her purse she asked me if I ever did security work before?

"No."

"You want to make some extra money on the side?"

"Hell yeah, what I gotta do?"

"Well we short one for security for the Lil Flip concert. You look pretty solid and like you can handle your weight. I just have to put you in a training class really quick so you can be certified than I can get you some gigs when some of these other clubs get short hand on body guards. That's if you think you can handle the position?"

"Trust I can hold my own they use to call me Mrs. Tyson because I have one hitter quitters. So yes, I can handle my own and would love to take the job." I get comfortable and wrapped my arm around her and went to sleep.

When I woke up it was about five in the evening. I had to look around to see where I was at because I do not remember going to sleep. As I am looking around I see MeMe purse and the night before came rushing back at me like a hangover. I gather myself together and walked out into the living room.

"Hello sleepyhead!'

"Hey ya'll, why no one woke me?"
"Well the kids did come in and try to wake you, but you were out. So, I got up and

we went to the store because we were bored and got some board games then the kids wanted McDonald's so we let you sleep. Your sister left she said she had some stuff to do today. Oh, and I paid her for babysitting."

"You didn't have to do all that but Thanks."

"No problem you hungry?"

"As a hostage."

"Here's ten go get something to eat. I didn't know when you would wake up, so we didn't get anything for you because it would have been cold."

"That's fine. Thank You."

I get in the shower, get dress and leave to get food. On my drive I was thinking to myself. What is going on? How I'd got into this? I really like her, but she is being too damn nice. What do she want from me? Oh well you know what Rain you only got one life so enjoy it and see where it goes.

When the day came for me to do security for Lil Flip I was nervous as hell. I got to the club the concert was held and we had a brief meeting of what is expected out of everyone and where our positions will be at. I got picked to be one of the three to secure the stage and be on stage with Lil Flip. My main goal that night was to do a great job and get an autograph for my son.

The concert was packed and like some stars he was late. When he does arrive, he is in a regular blacked out SUV and with a Constable escorting him into the parking lot. Lil Flip had the nerves to call one of us over to tell the owners he need $3,000 more or he is not coming in. The security guy taps me on the shoulder and tells me to follow him. When we get in he delivers the message and from the look on the owner face they were pissed. The owner counts out the cash and goes to the SUV and we follow behind. She pays him, and we escort him thru the back staircase and gets him upstairs.

I get to my station and the concert begins.
     All the ladies are screaming their lungs out and trying to pull at him. It was so exciting, and I felt like I was the one on stage they came to see. That's when I knew at that moment that I wanted to be in the spotlight. Lil Flip concert was the worst concert I have ever seen or heard about. He did two of his old song when he first came out and like four of T.I songs or a song he collaborated with. He passed out old ass CDs

and T-Shirts. He was on stage for about 20 minutes. Then it was up to the DJ to keep the party from flopping. He told each of us security on stage to pick out two chicks and send them upstairs. I don't know what he did or said to these ladies, but they came back downstairs pissed as hell and cussing him out talking about "He lost his mind and he don't know who they are and got them fucked up." I wanted to ask one of the girls so bad what happened but that would have been unprofessional.

After that I did a lot of bouncer work and was subbing for some of the regular guards. A regular night I get about $50-60. If it's a special event or celebrity I was getting $ 75 - $150. I took that job proudly and professionally, that is why I was getting so many gigs. I'm in charge of searching all the ladies because I was a female myself. Trust when I tell you though I

flirted with every girl that walks thru the door

and if she acted interested I got the number

before she leaves. I did work like this for about

two years.

The only other celebrity I got to escort was
Ja
Rule when him and Xscape did a free concert

for the Troops of Fort Hood on the fourth of

July. Last minute someone I did security with

before pulled me just to get Ja rule from the

stage to his car that was waiting for him, so he

can go. Xscape stuck around and signed

autographs for fans. I had my baby boy Eric

with me at the time and he had the biggest

crush on Tiny. When we finally got to where we

can get something signed. He lost his mind. He

told Tiny how much he loves her and to call

him and he gave her our house number. My son

took off his t shirt and asked them to sign it, first he had wanted them to sign his chest, we all laughed and told him no. I gave them my Freedom Iraqi hat to sign. They thought he was just the cutest thing. Little did they know this boy would not go outside or play for three whole days. He sat by that phone waiting on Tiny to call him.

MeMe had moved in with me a week after we met. With her being a stripper, promoter and waitress and me working at Wendy's and doing security at night. Our pockets stayed fat. One day we were having a conversation about where we from and I was telling her of how the killing is in Youngstown and why I ended up here. The thing that caught her attention the most was when I said that the only time I ever rode in a limo was for funerals.

That next month for my birthday she tells me to get dress, we go shopping for me some cloths and when it was time to step out. When I walked outside my house door there was a stretch blue limo with tinted windows and a sun roof waiting on us.

"What the hell, who limo?"

"Duh, it's in front of your house so it's for you."

"Are you fucking serious! Oh my God! I Love
You! "

"Love you too, now come on we have to pick up your friend Tiffany and get to the club we VIP tonight baby."

"Yes ma'am"
I acted just like a big kid. I was pushing buttons and hanging out the sun roof yelling what's up to the people looking at us stroll through neighborhoods. We get to my friend Tiffany

house picks her up and we then go to

Applebee's than to City Lights. I had the best

fun that night.

MeMe and me were together for a few

years off and on. We even try to have a baby

together and had a mutual friend as our sperm

donor. MeMe was facing a lot of issues and

stress, so she miscarried, and it tore us up. We

ended up splitting up and becoming friends.

Along with the miscarriage, meddling friends

and the big age difference because I was nine

years older than her. It all played a lot in our

break up.

After Meme I stayed single, but it did not

stop me from wanting love in my life. I was still

confused on who I really wanted to be. I did not

forget my main reason for moving to Texas and that was for a better life for my kids and to find love. By this time, I had moved into these apartments and was basically a hoe throughout cause anything that let me fucks and I didn't get a bad feeling about it, I fucked.

I did what I said I wasn't going to do down here and that's use sex as an escape for my pains and feelings. Again, I am back at square one, searching for who I am truly. I indulged in sex with both men and woman at this time. I was bashing in every direction. Females piss me off than its fuck females and then I

gets with a man. He pissed me off it was fuck men then I'm with a female. The whole time I am hating who I am and who I am becoming. I lost complete control and site of my purpose. I started hiding my emotions with crack, X pills, weed, cocaine and liquor. I was a total mess and still sleeping with everyone.

When me and the girl I was messing with at the time got into an argument over the pipe because she didn't like that I was smoking crack. We fought, and the pipe broke cutting my hand. I looked at the blood dripping out and at that moment I knew that I need to stop and get my shit together. So, I got rid of that girl and never picked up crack again. Now I was still doing the other drugs, but it's just something about being on crack that makes you look horrible to your friends and family. I thank God that I unlike most, had the will power to put it down and never pick it up again.   I knew that no matter what I am strong, wanted, loved and to be blessed. Those positive

thoughts kept me going for a long while.

GOING THRU THE MOTIONS

Now let's back track a little and clear some things up before we go on.

Studs do more than just eat out girls. I DO NOT PUT

MY MOUTH ON EVERYTHING OR

EVERYONE I STILL KISS MY KIDS AND

GRANDKIDS ON THE CHEEK!

So, since we are on the subject let's clear up some of the myths and misunderstandings in this chapter:

1. **Lipstick Lesbian or Femme** – loves to be feminine all the time and these are the ones that you cannot tell unless they tell you they gay.

   Mostly are Bi- sexual

2. **Bi Sexual** – Someone who enjoys sex with both male and female.

3. **Chapstick Lesbian** – they dress, like both stud and femme depending on their mood.

4. **Butch** – is the tough, make-up free and manly looking although they do not want to be with men.

5. **Stone Butch** – Her whole demeanor is to be the pleasure and giver. She thrives from making her lover reach her climax and by under no circumstances can you touch or handle her in a feminine manner what so ever.

6. **Boi Lesbian** – The one that do not hide they are a female but dress boyish.

7. **The Hasbian Lesbian** – Now when I heard of this crap I laughed really hard but here goes… A woman who once

identified as a lesbian or Bi but is now dating men.

8. **Fairies** – These are the studs who play stud but secretly sleeps with men.

9. **Studs** - These are the ones who walk, talk, dress, acts and carry themselves like a man.

10. **Dykes** – A woman who has never been with a man, wants to be a man, believe they are a man. This woman wears her strap - on 24/7 also prefers to be called him. They have changed their name and is known by a man's name. (Please do not ever call me this I despise this word.)

11. **Straight Lesbian** – This woman has never been with a man. Does not desire to be with a man in no shape form or

fashion. Get sick of the thought of being with a man. If a man said he slept with her it was to have a baby with her partner or he raped her. Period point blank.

Let us get into some of the dumbest questions I have heard in my life and what us lesbians are so sick and tired of hearing:

1. "But you don't look gay." – Didn't know it was a certain look let me go back and put my big "L"" on my forehead for ya.

2. "So you must really like girls?" Duh that's why I am gay.

3. "I thought you had a boyfriend before?" Yeah but I fucks a woman better.

4. "Wants to have a threesome with me

   and my girlfriend?" – Why? OH!

   Why? Do you men always asks us

   this? Then get mad if your girlfriend

   continues fucking me without you.

5. "You and your friend seems really
   close.

   Like ya'll have a lot of fun together
   can I
   chill with you two?"- Of course we

   look close. We fucking and no you

   can't chill with

   us.

6. "You're so sweet and cute, if I was

   gay I would date you." – Don't knock

   it till you try it sweetie.

7. Any questions about scissoring –

   There is more to sex than that

position. Men try scissoring with your

woman and tell me how

it feels.

8. 'You too cute to be gay." – My bad I

didn't know all gay people was ugly,

yet your ugly ass standing here

talking about what's cute.

9. Last but not least my all-time favorite:

YOU JUST HAVEN'T FOUND THE
RIGHT

DICK OR YOU JUST HAVEN'T BEEN
FUCKED PROPERLY BY A MAN
THAT'S

ALL.

Get the fuck out of here. What makes

some of ya'll men thinks this bullshit.

Clarification.
I am a freak and I have had some nice,

thick fat long dicks back in my day and

some wonderful men in my life that did

treated me like a queen along with all the

other women they were entertaining (not

all of them cheated) and guess what I'm

still GAY!

Quick questions folks: Why do men

think that raping a gay person will make

the person they raped straight?

Those men that rape gay men because

you mad they gay or for whatever

reason? Don't that make you angrily gay?

Why do people think Gay people in

general are child molesters? A sick

Mutha Fucker is a sick Mutha Fucker no

matter gay, white, black, dad, uncle,

brother, sister, mother. I'm just gonna

leave those questions there because to

me they speak for themselves.

As you can see for damn near every

name that they call us is a dumb ignorant

question that comes with it. Everything

is a title or a characterization with

everything we do. There is all kind of

racism that goes on in the world. I mean

let's name as many as we can name;

Religion

Color

Age

Sex

Sexuality

Money (yeah think about that

one.) Now you may wonder how the hell

money can be racism. Example: You have

a black man, and he make more money than the white man in the same department. If he was white he would not have a problem with him in that position (Double racism, if you ask me.). Not to mention black man got a degree, white man did not.

OK. Let's get back to the subject of the chapter, you know going through the motions. As I have grown older and have reached certain phases in my life so did my lesbianism. Yes, it truly is a phase some grow out of it, some grow into it and some try to see if that is for them. For some it is, for some it is not. All my close friends are straight. I am the only gay one in the bunch and I like to keep it that way.

Now let me explain some of the stud phases that

I have been through in my life.

Phase 1 -Understanding that you like women more than you should.

Phase 2 -Making the choice to fantasize about what I would do if I was to be with a woman.

Phase 3 -Accepting that I love women

Phase 4 -Get deep into Church. If no one can save me God can.

Phase 5 -Trying to understand why I do love woman and why He just didn't create me as a man.

Phase 6 -Fuck it I'm gonna follow the inside and forget what the outside looks like.

Phase 7 -Change entire wardrobe from women to men clothing. Even the socks and under wear.

Picked

up sports bra.

Phase 8 -Trying and wanting to be a man.

Phase 9 -Understanding that you have a

vagina and will never be a man. (I will never

alter my body

other than a tummy tuck.)

Phase 10 -Accepting who I am as a

person and not labeling myself because others

have a label for me.

Phase 11 –Learning and accepting that

God do not make mistakes and that means ME

as well. I am not a mistake. God made me who I

am and that is a Human being who loves her

friends and family. Who will give you the shirt

off her back if you needed it.

The woman who will have a place to sleep, eat

and a shoulder to cry on if you need it. A

woman who will fight you over your own kids if she feels you are mistreating or harming your child. A woman who wears her heart on her sleeve. A woman who loves to be loyal to her family and wants to be in love and married just like the next person. A woman who is a daughter, a mother, a grandmother, aunt, sister, cousin, niece, granddaughter and a friend. A woman that no matter how anyone looks at her or the many names she has been called or categorized in. I am still a child of GOD who prays, know her bible and who have a strong relationship with God.

It is not my fault that all you choose to see me as a woman who sleeps with women.

Can I get an AMEN!

Christian folks, Yeah there's a lesson for you too.

Please stop beating us up with your words and bibles.

That is not how you get a person to believe your version of Gods plan for their soul. Let me help you out.

Get to know the person, fellowship with the person, make them feel as if they belong there, comfort them if they look like they need comforting and do not be fake about it. No one wants to feel like everyone is staring at or talking about them. Ya'll stop doing that and stop focusing your sermons on homosexuality the minute a gay person tries to fellowship with you a couple of Sundays. Talking about one thing then start saying God put it in their spirit to say this and that. With the whole time you constantly looking over at me locking eyes. Stop it! You made that choice for the sermon because you still looking back into your written sermon trying to convince me God sent this message thru you to me. Again, we are human and have feelings too. You may learn something about yourself from a person like me. Hope you just learned something with my book.

A lot of us do not want to feel the way we feel and when we come for answers or relief. Most Christians turn into a wolf in sheep clothing's to us. Wondering why we never came back to church and then will have the nerve to say we didn't want our soul saved. How could we when you treated us like a demon needing to be casted out of us instead of a lost soul that needs saving. Again, God words will speak to a person on its own. God do not need your help other than to be a Vessel.

And this is coming from the Gay one. LOL

A person may think their own ways are right, but

the Lord weighs the heart. **<u>Proverbs 21:2</u>**

P.S There is only heterosexual and homosexual stop making up all these names for something you have no clue of or afraid of. It's confusing to others not us.

1st Corinthian 13 – hint, hint

WHERE AM I NOW?

Let's see its 2012 and by this time I had been through three whole relationships with some very interesting women.

The first was with Shun. Shun was a sexy yellow bone, 4'11 a big booty and a smile. We met at the gay club where me and a homeboy went there to handle some business from our job for the night before. Once we were done I decided to chill a little and see if I could pull something for the night. The DJ was live, and the club was jumping. I worked my way to the dance floor and danced with everyone who let me dance with them. Finally, I put on my game face and approach this one girl who I noticed was staring at me. When I began to walk up is when I noticed her little friend. I thought to myself damn I want her. I introduced myself

and asked if they wanted to dance. They said

yeah, and both took me back to the dance floor.

While both is dancing with me I am putting it

on thick trying to get into bed with them both

together.   After a few songs we head on over

to the bar and I offer to buy our drinks. Shun

sent her friend to get our drinks and I gave her

the money. The moment

she left.

"Your friend seems pretty messed up. You
good?"

"Yeah, I'm good and she is twisted. Guess she'll

be spending the night, but I knew that anyways

when she

wanted to go out."

"So, is ya'll going to your house after here?'

"Yeah. Why?"

"Shit I'm trying to go home with you. Your friend cool and all and I know she likes me, but it's you I'm trying to get with."

"You're cute, but what makes you think I want you to go home with me?"

"Two reasons. One you gonna need someone to help you get your friend in and out the car. She a big girl and you a lil one, so you can use the help. And two.

You

haven't said No yet."

We chuckled. She smiles, and her friend returns with our drinks. We all engaged in a conversation when I guess one of her friend songs come on. We hit the dance floor again. By the second song Homegirl was ready to throw up. In my head, I'm like "Yes!" So as you can guess. I helped her get her friend into the vehicle and we headed to Shun house.

After getting her friend on the couch. We

laugh and talk trash about her friend because

she didn't know her head from her toe. Once

her friend went to sleep we started talking

and she was like.

"I can't believe I let you come here."

"Well I swear I'm no rapist or murderer."

"Well let me get you a cover."

"What? You not leaving me out here with

Drunkin Donuts. She might rape me in my

sleep, you know she want me. I promise I will

be a perfect gentleman and won't try to touch

you at all. Hell, I'll even sleep on top

of the cover."

"Whatever Rainy, I swear you touch me you

will be walking home where ever the fuck you

live at." "Aww. Don't be like that. There's

nothing wrong with a onenight stand. Plus, you remembered my name so we

good."

"Wait here till I get dress into my comfy cloths."

"Yes Ma'am."

She disappears to the back and comes and gets me when she get her night cloths on, which was some booty shorts and a tank top. The booty shorts really brought out the shape, roundness and softness of her ass. I was sitting on the couch when she said, "Come on." We go to her bedroom. I took off my shoes and climbed in the bed. We talked till we fell asleep. The next morning, I jumped up and shouted. "Damn I was supposed to get my kids at 7. Shit, my sister is going to flip out.

Shun was in the shower. When she comes out. I was looking into my phone to call my sister Zetta.

When I looked up Oh my God. She is beautiful.

"See told you I would be a perfect gentleman."

"Umhmm"

"What? Did I do something?"

"Naw, you good. I'm just fucking with you. You're sweet and cute. I just don't sleep with everyone nor on the first night."

"So, you saying you want to sleep with me? If so that can definitely be arranged."

She laughs. "Who knows what may happen later." "Umhmm. Ain't that what you just said to me?"

"You a mess, come on so I can take you home. Where do you live at?'

"In Heights."

I used the bathroom and we gets into the vehicle and she drive me home. On the ride she finally tells me about her kids and how they in Dallas with her Mom for the summer.

Once we get to my destination. I thank her gives her a hug and a kiss on the check then asked her for her number. She gives it to me, I call it.

"Just want to make sure you're giving me
the right

number."

She laughs, and she pulls off. When I get into the house. Me and my sister got into a big heated argument. By this time, I had pocket dialed her and she heard everything.

Next thing I know she calls me and was like.

"You and your kids can come stay with me for the summer, till you get a place. I got plenty of room. I am

turning around now."

"What?"

"This Shun I am coming back to get you and the

kids. I heard everything. Fuck your

sister."

"You sure? I got three big kids. They no babies."

"I'm outside come on we will get ya'll stuff later."

"OK, Here I come."

So, me and the kids moved in with Shun that next day.

We were together off and on for four years. Got matching tattoos on our forearm. I got her middle name on my neck.

How I fucked that up?

On her birthday I gathered 31 pennies that had the year from her birth till that current year. I glued each penny on a cardboard paper. I named each penny as a reason to why she was born. I made it into a book. When she got to the last page. It said to turn around and when she did I was on a knee with a ring asking her to marry me.

She said, Yes.

Now a few years after and a break up I wanted to give Shun a surprised wedding. So, I worked like a dog trying to stack this money. Focusing so much on a wedding that I neglected my woman when she needed me mentally and spiritually and to listen to her when she was having a bad day. I used to be a hard person to talk to and would not listen. It was my way or the highway. Being this type of person help me lose a very good woman to another.

I learned that lesson.

The next few relationships only lasted a year or less. The first time me and Shun broke up it was a planned temporary thing because her military husband was back from overseas and even though they split up. It was not legally so he had to come back to the house. The second time, I had moved out completely and we were still friends plus we have grown a relationship with each other kids. I started dating this Nurse at my job. I know bad move.

 Well Shun worked at the same place as well. That was not the problem. The problem was that even though me and Shun was not together, we still did stuff with each other kids.

Now before I get into what happened with this woman, let me explain something.

You have these types of woman that seems normal and OK. But in reality, they are attention getting, crazy ass and psychotic people. We all have had our experience with people like this. I call them Banana Rama.

Ok back to the story.

Me and this Nurse was cool until I noticed some of her crazy coming out. We used to get into a disagreement and before I know it. BAM! This Heffa done passed out and fell straight back.

The first time she did it I freaked out and right before I called 911 she wakes up and didn't want to go to the hospital. I did not catch it at first that when she "so calls" faints it's never forwards that she falls. It's always backwards and always when we are having a disagreement. Never any other time. She even

faked a seizure a couple times before. I nipped

that in the bud after the second time when I just

threw a big cup of ice water in her face. She

woke up then, with the quickness. Now we all

worked at the same nursing facility and it's

getting close to Christmas time. So, everyone

picking up hours and working for their kids.

Me and Banana Rama worked the graveyard

shift. This particular night Shun picked up a

shift.

Now with the night shift. The dumpster is far

from the building and is in a not so well-lit area.

The rule is that since it's only four aides on the

floor for nights. We take our trash out with a

buddy and the nurse from the shift before picks

who is buddies for the night. Me and Shun is

buddies for the night. So long story short.

Banana Rama and the laundry lady was good friends.

When it was time for us to take our trash out.

Me and Shun notices how the laundry lady was all in our mouth and trying to be in our conversation. Now let us not forget that Shun is 4'11 and I am 5'8 so I bended down to talk to the top of Shun head and said. "This bitch looking for trouble watch she go tell that woman some bullshit and all we are talking about is what we gonna get the kids for Christmas, so we won't get the same stuff." We laughed and went back into work.

No less than an hour later.

This crazy woman went to her car, took her scrub shirt off and came back into the building with a baseball bat and a big ass butcher knife.

She came running towards me yelling.

"I'm gonna fucking kill you." Man, I took off running backwards and ran right into the nurse's station area desk. I looked back to see why I was not moving. By this time a co working stepped in front of me and started yelling at her to think of her daughter to stop being stupid.

Thank God she did not harm me and ran out the building when she heard the sirens because someone dialed 911.

I had to get a police escort just to get my stuff that I had at her house and they charged her with terroristic threats.

What do I do next? I moved back in with Shun and we lasted another year and a half before I lost her for good.

After all this I moved to Copperas Cove and started working at another nursing facility.

I had been single for a little and was really trying to just stay away from relationships in general. So, I thought.

At this Nursing home I was like fresh meat. I was flirting, and they are flirting back. I remember me, and a coworker was cleaning a patient. When we got done cleaning our mess. This girl grabs my arm and pulled me into a closet and kissed the shit out of me. I was stunned and flattered at the same time. All me and that girl ever did was kiss and she would grind on me when she came to visit but I was adamant about being single, so I never took it no farther.

So, in my head I wanted to try something different and it was this white girl at the job that we had become very close, but she moved to Virginia. I admit I wanted to see how much game I had with the different race. Well my game was too damn good cause this girl and her daughter had moved back to Texas in with me and again I wanted to get marry.

This is when I started to notice that God do give us signs before we make any big steps in our lives. We just got to learn to recognize them, figure out what our purpose is and follow the Lords lead.

I had so many signs not to marry that girl, yet when I decided not to go through with it and I sat her down and told her. Of course, there was an argument and crying. I leave to clear my head and sneak and smoke a blunt because she was so against me being high and drinking. I was sneaking every blunt and drink while she was at work. So, you can say I was cheating on her with controlled substances.

When I returned to the house she was laying in the bed with her wedding dress on, flowers and all. Looking pathetic. Like a typical butt head. I felt bad and married her anyways.

Eleven months later she gets pissy ass drunk (go figure) acted a complete fool, damaged some of our belongings right before she got on the plane to go to her parents. I never saw her again.

Till this day that woman hates my guts. Wish I could tell you why. But I do not know. Shit happens oh well.

So, what did I learn from all this and where am I know?

- I must be a better partner if I want a better partner.

- Listen to understand and not to respond.

- Pay attention to her body language and gestures, they are a cry for fixing or helping her.

- Money is the main reason for most divorces. Do not let it be a reason for yours.

- Be patient and WAIT. Love will find you in the best way.

- Finally: If I really look around it may just be right up under my nose.

Which leads us to the next chapter.

NOW THE JOURNEY
REALLY

BEGINS

Once I said my good-byes a year after me and L.A divorce. I got on the road to head back to Texas alone. It was my first time driving this far especially by myself. I knew that I wanted to take this road trip as a time to reflect and get my act together and get my wife back. On that 20 hours ride I got to see some great sights and really got the feel of being a loner. Not having to answer to no one.

No one to take care of or look after. I was beginning to feel at peace. There is nothing but the road and me.

When I got to my baby momma Shela house I was energized as hell and was no ways tired. I couldn't wait to see my Texas family. Shela had a room with a small half bathroom in it all set up for me. I unloaded my stuff from the car and relaxed with some of the family.

The next day I got up and got me a job at Subway and started making plans on my next move

A.W.R.P Another Where's Rain Production. What is A.W.R.P? Well it's a small indie company that provides DJ, photography, video graphing, directing, managing, producing, promoting and song writing services.

I threw myself into A.W.R.P. I took every dime after I paid my little bit of bills and Shela. I got business cards, my LLC and began scouting for talent. I ended up meeting a guy who did almost all the same work I was trying to get off the ground. I will say that I met some wonderful people working with this man. We did work for a promotor where we took pictures at

the

Rickey

Smiley show held in Killeen, Texas. I also met my hand model for the book cover Ms. Sasha Mone' and a couple of guys who formed a group that consists of five men and two teenagers called Unique Sound. These guys were very talented, and I was amazed at the different creative styles that they had and how they were able to come together musically. They had it all except a good manager.

After a couple of other jobs with the guy everyone decided that working with him was more beneficial for him then us, so we started linking up and build a business relationship with each other.

After a couple of meetings with the fellas I brought the idea of adding a girl to the group for a little edge and flavor to the group and I knew just the woman. Mizz. LayDee, I knew her since she was a teenager because she one of Shela's best friends and I heard her rap when she was like fifteen and I told her back then when I get to where I wanted to be I was coming for her. Well ten years later, here I come, and she was ready.

I introduced her to the fellas and it was on. They loved her. We worked our ass off. I was on their ass every chance I got. I am a tough business woman. I believe in morals, respect and work ethics. I am also a perfectionist. We were always rehearsing and recording. I sat and watched each member closely, so I could see where they may improve individually in order to be a great whole. All the while we were growing as a family.

I was promoting the hell out of A.W.R.P so, the DJ services and the gigs were rolling in. To help give the group some exposure and real stage time, some of my shows I would have them as a special guest and let them perform two to three songs for the crowd. This really did help the group and me as their manager out because two of them had stage fright.

We finally picked out three songs for performance songs and recorded them. Now it's time to get an album complete. By then the group had made me an honorary member and I contributed two songs to the album. I did "2 Damn Broke" which is a song I done years ago, and we redid it some and put it on the album, and I wrote the words to "Waiting" a love song that the singer of the group needed for his part on the album.

That was a song I had wrote for L.A after our divorce.

The leader of the group was also acting manager and co-producer to the group. Together we put every dime we could into equipment, gas, food, etc. so everyone was comfortable and had everything they needed. We made sure if you didn't have a ride to rehearsal we came and got you. Whatever it

took to get

U.S where we need to be. We started getting

compliments and a few more invites to shows

and contests.

Two of us had to make a trip to Florida

for some personal business. It was my first time

going to Florida plus I drove most of the way

because he had C.Q when he got off and we had

to hit the road. Sorry forgot to mention that four

of the members were Soldiers in the Army.

When it was my turn to rest I was on the phone

scheduling more shows and we had got the

chance to get three spots for the South by

Southwest event in Austin, Texas. For those

who do not know what that is let me tell you; it

is a musical festival for independent artists,

Promotors, Managers and Scouters, They all

come to these events looking for the next big hit. So many musical artist and some other celebrities come to this event. It is a great opportunity for artists to get their music out to the right people, exposure and you also learn a lot about the business side of music.

Getting into SXSW was a big deal to us. It was like a 50% chance of getting that big record deal. We had less than four months to get hotels, album pressed and transportation ready. The leader of the group decided that we will have a unique uniform style to us , therefore, we wore different color army fatigue pants and some special made shirts with the album cover on the front and our stage names on the back plus the shirts glowed in the dark it was nice.

With the album being almost complete I decided to give the group an album release concert, so I looked all around Killeen for a

venue. I came across a place on the web called

The Love Lounge. It was in the 440 Plaza on

Fort Hood Road. I went to find the location and

see if it was a place I would like. I had called

and set up an appointment. Once I got there I

could not find which building it was, so I

walked into this place where I saw someone

walking in.

"Hello, I am looking for The Love

Lounge, can you tell me where

it is?"

"Yeah it's right next door."

"OK. Thank you. Hey, if you don't

mind me asking what you got going on over

here. I never seen this part of the Plaza open

before."

"Me and a bout four of my colleagues is opening up a comedy spot to bring underground comedy to the community. We are calling it Laugh It

Up Comedy

Lounge."

"Wow that's great all black owned and comedy yes thanks for bringing it to town instead of us always having to go to Austin, San Antonio or Houston. Do you

have a DJ already?"

"For our first night yes and we are having Sheryl Underwood but we do not have a house DJ."

Before he could say anything else. "I DJ." And

I handed him my card.

After briefly speaking about me and what I do. I continued my original mission and went next door to the Love Lounge and set up a day for the group album release show.

Two days later Mr. Daryll from Laugh It Up Comedy Lounge called me to come in and shadow the DJ for Sheryl Underwood so I will know how to set up and what to do for a show. I must admit, I only did bars, clubs and house parties. DJing for a comedy show was something totally different. I was learning a new level of DJing that I never knew, and I was like a kid in the toy store. I watched and observed everything around me. I studied the DJ and he was giving me some

pointers. I watched the audience reaction to everything.

I wanted to be the best and I had one night to learn what

I needed to learn. It was either sink or swim in my eyes. So, I swam my ass off.

Sheryl Underwood was wonderful. She was so down to earth and loved to cuss. She also can drink some of my so-called drinking friends under the table. She was ordering drinks for her and a member of the audience like it was part of her act. The club even named a special drink after her. She was amazing I tell you and she made sure she spoke or shake everyone hands that got her attention. I love seeing celebrities that do not forget that the only difference between me and you are the media exposure and money. We are all human. I commend the celebrities like that and I met a lot of celebrities in my life so far that are like that in

person.

From that point on I was the house DJ for
Laugh

It Up Comedy Lounge. Now believe it or not I
was
DJing with a Gateway Desktop computer and a

Numark DJ party mixer. It's a mixer for

beginners. It was all I could afford at the time

even though I am a higher-level DJ. I made

lemonade out of lemons. I thank the Lounge for

everything they taught me and the patience

they had with me when my equipment might

give me a little trouble. I had got the great

pleasure to DJ for some wonderful and great

comedians let me name some:

Lavell Crawford

Gary "G Thang" Johnson from the hit
show

Grown Folks.

J J Williamson
Rich Williams

Canice

Barbara Carlyle

Mope Williams

Eric Green

And none of the Williams are related.

After being in the comedy scene and seeing

what really goes on with the comedy world, I

wanted my hands in it some more. I became the

road manger for a good friend from school in

Ohio who does comedy, Eboni

"Eye

Holla"

Gordon, and the leader of Unique Sound had a

solider friend who is getting started with

comedy. So now A.W.R.P has three clients and

is a house DJ for the Comedy Lounge. I was on top of the world. Every comedian I was able to get to sit down and talk to I did. I would ask questions that would help my comedians be better in what they do. The one who talked to me like an auntie and gave me so much insight in what I was doing, and my comedians was Barbara Carlyle. She taught me so much in twelve minutes.

I think I got about three hours of sleep a day because I was so excited all the time and praying I did not want to miss a beat. With every Friday, Saturday and Sunday at the comedy club the rest of the week was rehearsal, recording and scheduling. I was on such a rush and high. I would not realize that I haven't ate some days. My baby momma's Shela and Ann really stepped up with me and made sure I didn't forget some things and always gave their insights to our music. When they found out I didn't eat one day they got into my ass and made sure I had one good meal a day.

Thanks ladies, I was on it. Everything I did and breathed was about A.W.R.P and Unique Sound. I was on a high that no one could get me down from. I felt great and so alive about my passion and dreams coming true.

Now it's time for our SXSW shows and because I had to get replaced for that weekend that was my end of DJing at Laugh It Up Comedy Lounge. I had added our comedian Eye Holla to the bill. She opened for us so, we had a complete show for our SXSW appearance. I got the room for us females and the guys shared a room. We had a last-minute guest which caused some trouble with the group along with all the personal stuff we all combined with business no wonder. What was supposed to be a great step in our career became a

Disaster.

At the last minute the song we were supposed to do, got changed and they added a piece to the beginning with no type of rehearsal, one of the members quit the day of us heading out to Austin and I broke my ankle missing my step off a curb passing out flyers at SXSW. I tore all my muscle and ligaments off my ankle bone. I was so doped up from the medications they gave me, and I was so hungry that I cooked some

Ramen Noodles in the coffee pot. Eye Holla and Mizz. LayDee clowned me so bad and videotaped me cooking it that it made over a thousand views on Eye Holla page. That was my eye opener for a YouTube channel.

Our pressed album was not ready in time so two of the member had to drive 4 hours to pick them up during SXSW. During one of the events the radio personal was talking to everyone about BMI and ASCAP and how important it is to have. With her providing this information was how I found out that the leader of the group had registered with BMI and ASCAP already and the album we just done is copywritten under his name and production company, so if anything was to become of the album it all was going to his bank account and we would not know a thing unless he told us. All our hard work and music gone like that. I felt like a failure to myself and Mizz. LayDee because I brought her in. I pulled the members who showed the most dedication and drive aside and informed them of what was going on. When we got back from SXSW I called a meeting and removed myself from the group as a member and their manager. We all have not been the same since and the group completely split up. I still work with one of the former member Big Slim Baby, Mizz. LayDee, Eye Holla and Steve O our two comedians.

So now it's back to the drawing board with me and I needed to come up with something fast so the name RainyRain and A.W.R.P would not die, and people forget about me. I had got me another job and by this time Shela was pregnant with her third child and this pregnancy had her hormones all out of whack and we got into a big argument. Me and Shela never argued nor been upset with each other so I decided to move with Ann till she had the baby. That did not last long neither, it was too crowded plus me and Ann as usual are bickering, so to avoid any more stress and headache than what I was already going thru, so for the next five months I made myself homeless, slept in my car and saved all my money for my own place and studio equipment. I got a storage unit to put all my stuff in I was getting together to move into my own. By the beginning of the summer 2017 I had got me a two bedroom apartment in Harker Heights, Texas. I made the second bedroom a studio and created Da RainyRain Show where I play old school hip hop rap music and talk about the changes in rap era. I had special segments called Can You Hang where I get a local young school rapper and they freestyle to a surprise old school instrumental and see if they can hang through the whole song. I also had Did You Know where you got some old school true Hip Hop facts. I would go

Facebook live every Thursday for two hours. I had Mizz. Laydee as a co-host for the first two shows. My kids and friends all made some type of appearance on the show. I launched it off January 2018. I even have a YouTube channel for the show.

Everything was going great. I had my own place and equipment was coming to me so easy. It was like

God wanted me to go in this direction. For the first time in my life I truly trusted God and where he was leading me. I stayed prayed up. I did so much research and learning for what I am getting myself into. I remember a family member once told me that if I don't believe and invest in myself, how can I expect anyone else to do it for me. I thrive off those words and I made myself locally known in Texas.

I got a little bit of exposure when I did a video that I wrote, directed and produced myself call: "I Get

High". What I did was took R Kelly song I Believe I Can

Fly and made it a weed song. I posted the video on a

Sunday morning at 6 a.m. by 9 a.m. I got an email from YouTube and R Kelly's publisher stating that I cannot get paid for the views, but it will have commercials and be added to the side line recommendations when you look up R Kelly songs. That was all I need to get my motor running and to know that this is for me and the direction I must go in.

Da Rainyrain Show was growing and I felt like I needed to do something more with the show. I set a meeting with my Program Consultant and we discussed the show having a segment that was more geared towards some type of informational or entertainment news. Once she said that I knew exactly who to bring into the program. Ms. Marsha Trowel. She was a former co-worker who love watching all the Love and Hip Hop shows and Black Ink. She had a sense of humor and was very loud and outspoken. She was perfect. I scheduled a meeting with her and we talked about our ideas and what she wanted to name it. I gave her all creative, research and writing credits to her fifteen-minute segment. She calls all those shows her

Ratchet People
TV, so that's what we named it Ratchet People Talk with Marsha. That was it I had a complete show. My main goal was to always have and do something different, I wanted the show to be as real as possible and I did not want it to be scripted so the only thing that was written for the show was the did you know facts, the topic of the day and an outline of what we are to talk about during the show.

My brother Mike always told me to never get comfortable with your current situation and that's what

I did I got comfortable. The show started running into problems. People were not showing up, technical issues along with me dealing with my manic depression I was on my way to the end of a ticking time bomb. I had been so busy and was working in such a routine manner that it build up on me and I did not face some of my reality in my life like I should have.

I had a break down. I felt like it was all too much, and I did not want to do this no more nor did I want to be here on this earth anymore.

I called Ann and she stayed with me for two days and helped me through the depression stage and suicidal thoughts.

Once that was over I got back on track and began upgrading my equipment. I moved the show to

Fridays and for one hour instead of two. I had noticed that more people were on Facebook on Fridays and the majority of our viewers were watching the show after it aired. I was pleased but not content with the direction of the show.

To get a better creative feel for myself I moved

the studio to the master bedroom and gave the

show a whole new look. I have set 1 where I

open the show with the show banner in the

background and my turntables, then there is set

2 where we have the A.W.R.P name and logo as

the backdrop and where Ratchet People Talk

with Marsha do her segment at and lastly I have

set 3 where I have my Ohio State and Cleveland

Cavaliers banners as the backdrop to represent

where I come from. This Master

bedroom now looks like a live

studio. I got an upgraded camera to shoot our

scenes. It was all I ever wanted and needed.

Now that everything was into place and

all new equipment I was ready to take Da

RainyRain Show to another level. So, I thought

like I said I got comfortable. Our show was interrupted with digital pixel problems, internet shutting down during the middle of the show and me and my viewers are getting upset and restless. A few guests had to reschedule or did not show up it was beginning to be a mess. So, I cancelled that next week show to get the errors fixed and get back into the groove of things. It still took a month and an upgrade with internet service to get it together but now my show is being cut after twenty minutes. I felt like Facebook was messing with me and that I had something big that they don't want out. I was too real. The first step was muting almost all my shows, even though I will say several times during the show and put into the title that I do not own the rights to the music and let's not forget I am a registered DJ.

I still was muted and had went back and forth disputing it with Facebook and Sony Music about it. I could not win I had to stop playing

Sony Music on the show. I was lost, what do I do now? Again, I had to cancel a show and redirect my whole show and concept. I wanted to stay in the music field and since I was self-funded the music was my commercial breaks in between discussions. I decided to start featuring local unsigned artists as my music to the show and started interviewing anyone who had a Cd, Book or doing something positive in the entertainment industry.

I hit it! The show started getting more subscribers and more compliments on what I was doing with the show. Yet again here come Facebook messing with my show someway somehow. Going live was not an option anymore. I was too afraid of losing my fans.

So, I began prerecording the shows and switched to YouTube with no set day of release of interviews so now my fans can watch whatever, whenever. I show so much more creative side to my work and what I can do, and the video graphing is so natural to me and now my goal is to be a radio personality, novelist and video/movie director and film all my own stuff. I completely lost interest in writing, directing and producing music now. My passion is still there for

DJing and my love for music. It is just that God showed me along my journey that I have grown as an individual and businesswoman.

The more I tried to stay in the music area the more I got pulled into another direction. When the time came God gave me the notion and drive to finish this book and take another step to another level in my life.

So I did.

UNIQUE SOUND

Page

INTRODUCING ………

RICH WILLIAMS
APRIL 15, 2017

A NIGHT OF FUN AND LAUGHTER

A.W.R.P brings you a great show like no other with live R&B performances as well as some great comedians AND PLENTY OF SPECIAL GUESTS to tickle your funny bone and lift your spirits.

Our headliner Rich you have seen him on "The Real" and at The Improv" So come on out and enjoy your Easter weekend with us.

Advance tickets are at The Love Lounge/Phileos in the 440 plaza or by calling A.W.R.P @ (330) 559-2320.

A.W.R.P, Goodnite Music and The Love Lounge
Presents....
Aries R us and A Night of Fun and Laughter

APRIL 14th & 15th

THE LOVE LOUNGE

868 S. FT. HOOD ST. KILLEEN, TX

BOTH SHOWS IN ADVANCE $18

APRIL 14 - $8/ADVANCE - $10/DOOR

APRIL 15 - $10/ADVANCE - $12/DOOR (formal wear)

WITH COMEDIAN EYE HOLLA FROM THE IMPROV AND THE MOVIE

"THE REFRACTOR" &

YOUR HOST K TOWNS OWN BIG SLIM BABY

MUSICAL ENTERTAINMENT BY DJ STAN IN THE MIX WITH LIVE

TAPING & PERFORMANCES FROM UNIQUE SOUND AND **MANY**

MORE SPECIAL GUESTS!

Tickets on sale now @ the Love Lounge or by calling A.W.R.P @

(330) 559-2320 FOR INFO.

DARK SKINNED 4 LIFE
Live in ATLANTA
Live in ATLANTA
Live in ATLANTA
To the boss
it will of chael
FOLLOW ME ON TWITTER TWITTER/@2GTHANG
LIKE ME ON FACEBOOK FACEBOOK/GARYGTHANG
EMAIL GTHANG5000@AOL.COM

LAUGH IT UP
COMEDY LOUNGE
202-796-8594
WWW.KILLEENLAUGHLOUNGE.COM
874 S. FORT HOOD ST.
INSIDE THE 440 PLAZA COURTYARD
Laugh it up COMEDY Lounge
LAVELL CRAWFORD
2 ITEM MINIMUM
OR $10 SURCHARGE
G/A $30
PREFERRED SEATING $35
LIMITED SEATING
FEBRUARY 10TH
DOORS OPEN AT 7:00PM
SHOW STARTS AT 8:00PM
DOORS OPEN AT 10:00PM
SHOW STARTS AT 10:30PM
FEBRUARY 11TH
DOORS OPEN AT 7:00PM
SHOW STARTS AT 8:00PM
DOORS OPEN AT 10:00PM
SHOW STARTS AT 10:30PM
FEBRUARY 12TH
DOORS OPEN AT 6:30PM
SHOW STARTS AT 7:30PM
TICKET OUTLETS:
PRESTIGE BEAUTY SALON
254-634-2348
GAY'S HOUSE OF BEAUTY
254-699-6935
SWEET FACTORY
254-616-1975

043
SATURDAY, 7 JAN. 2017
DOORS: 6:00 PM | SHOW: 7:00PM
LAUGH IT UP
COMEDY LOUNGE
PRESENTS
BARBARA CARLYLE
& FRIENDS
SATURDAY
JAN. 7TH, 2017
DOORS: 6:00 PM | SHOW: 7:00 PM
LAUGH IT UP COMEDY LOUNGE
874 S. FORT HOOD ST., KILLEEN, TX 76541

EYE HOLLA

COAST 2 COAST LIVE
INTERACTIVE EVENTS
330
DTH
3/17/2006

EPILOGUE

When I started on this book it was a couple years after moving to Texas in 2002 and Lord knows I've been wanted to finish this book. I wanted this to have a happy ending because even though I'm forty-three years old I still believe in happy endings and Love. So, when I just couldn't get the motivation or will to complete this. I prayed and asked for guidance. He showed me that I could not finish it until I go thru some more trials in my life because there were so many lessons I had to learn before I share my life and be used as a vessel. I also had to find out who my true wife to be is....

As I was walking through the walkway at work one day. I was looking at the pictures on everyone's cubicles. You see I love pictures plus I'm nosey.

As I was speaking to a coworker a picture caught my eye. Well hell she caught my eyes. It was like I was in a room all alone and there is no one in the room but us, our eyes connect, and we are staring each other dead in the eyes. The crazy part was that the first thought that came to my mind was: Hey there goes your wife.

I'm like, what the hell! By this time, I realized that I stop walking and is staring at this picture. I wipe my eyes and for some reason I could not turn my head and the person who desk it was is talking to me.

After wiping my eyes. I lock back dead set on the picture and this time I can see only the woman face; the next thought was: There goes your wife. Again. I am like what the hell! I drop the picture. Yeah, I had picked it up off their desk in had it in my hand without even noticing I have done this.

While the picture was on the floor I see her whole body and there were three other girls in this picture, but I only see her. Once I saw how sexy and beautiful she was that last thought was: Yeah that's gonna be your wife! I picked up the picture and handed to my coworker told her my bad and rushed to my desk. I have not been able to get this woman out my head since. All I kept thinking was: I got to know who she is. I must find out who this woman is. So, I did. We talked and got to know each other a little bit but she was badly damaged and needed to focus on herself and find who she is and what really makes her happy, so we just stopped talking.

Where am I on love, well I'm content.

I now know what I want, who I am and to

be patient. I wants to date and actually grow to

know a person ONE day at a time and one day

fall in love. After 7 years of being single, I want to

date so I am.

Now we are at the end of my story.

You may wonder after all that. I'm still a lesbian

so why call it Tha Recovering Lesbian.

Well to prove a point:

The moment you saw the word **Recovering**

you thought of the definition: **to return to normal**

state of health, mind or strength. Or of a person

being well again

.

Guess what? **Recovering** also has another definition to the word which also means:

To find or regain possession of. To regain control of (oneself or of a physical or mental state.) I found and regain possession of myself and who I am as a person and that's RainyRain McQueen. So, basically in the end a relationship is a relationship no matter if it's man/man, man/woman or woman/woman. It is all about two people who made the consensus decision to live, laugh and love each other for as long as they can through everything they can endure, TOGETHER.

God bless, and I hope you enjoyed my story.

Now it is time for me to use the first definition of

Recovering for Love in my life.

FOR BOOKING:

Recoveringsecrets19@Gmail.Com

As I walk through the shadows of death
I shall fear no evil.